HOW TO PASS

SECONDARY SCHOOL SELECTION TESTS

HOW TO PASS
SECONDARY SCHOOL SELECTION TESTS

Mike Bryon

KOGAN
PAGE

Publisher's note
Every possible effort has been made to ensure that the information contained in this book is accurate at the time of going to press, and the publishers and authors cannot accept responsibility for any errors or omissions, however caused. No responsibility for loss or damage occasioned to any person acting, or refraining from action, as a result of the material in this publication can be accepted by the editor, the publisher or the author.

First published in Great Britain in 2004

Kogan Page Limited
120 Pentonville Road
London N1 9JN
United Kingdom
www.kogan-page.co.uk

© Mike Bryon, 2004

The right of Mike Bryon to be identified as the author of this work has been asserted by him in accordance with the Copyright, Designs and Patents Act 1988.

British Library Cataloguing in Publication Data

A CIP record for this book is available from the British Library.

ISBN 0 7494 4217 4

Typeset by Saxon Graphics Ltd, Derby
Printed and bound in Great Britain by Bell & Bain, Glasgow

Contents

Acknowledgements

I owe thanks to my daughter Hope for commenting on much of the content of this book while taking tests to secure a secondary school place.

1

Notes for parents

Testing for secondary school places

Entrance exams have been a feature of the admission policy of independent schools for many years. They have also become common in the state sector, especially with oversubscribed schools. To get a feel for the extent of testing, I reviewed the entries for over 530 schools in the 2002 edition of the *London School Guide* published by Mitchell Beazley. The guide lists both independent and state schools and I found that around 30 per cent of this sample rely on entrance tests at some stage of the admissions process.

The effect of such widespread testing is that very many children must take an exam when applying to the school of their choice. Children who make multiple applications may face a whole series of exams for the different schools to which they have applied.

This book is intended to help children prepare for secondary school entrance exams. It contains over 600 practice questions split between three main types of exam papers: mathematics, verbal reasoning and non-verbal reasoning. In Chapter 5, answers and a large number of explanations are provided.

The best sort of practice that you can provide for your child is on material that is very similar to the questions in the real test. Before you use this book, try to establish the type of question contained in the real test. Take care to ensure that the practice material provided here is relevant to the challenge faced by your child. I have tried to include material that is relevant to most tests and will benefit most children. This may mean, however, that not all the material is relevant to your child's situation. So seek to select the most appropriate material in terms of both the level of difficulty and question type.

If your child has a disability that will affect his or her ability to complete the exam then be sure to inform the school at the first opportunity. In many instances extra time is allowed or the exam is organized in a different way to accommodate your child's needs.

How practice can help

Schools use entrance exams for a variety of reasons. Some use them to select the more able children and in this context the exam may be a straight competition for places. Others use an exam to ensure that the intake is representative of all abilities. In this context it is possible that a higher-scoring child will not gain a place while a lower-scoring child will.

Practice helps, whatever the purpose of the exam. If the test is used to stream children then practice will help make sure that your child is familiar with the questions and more confident about the test. A lack of familiarity, nervousness or a lack of confidence will result in a lower score and could mean that your child does not demonstrate his or her true potential, making an assessment inaccurate.

In a competitive situation parents can do much to help their child. Systematic preparation is the key and it can help ensure that your child gains the best possible score.

Practice helps because it means that your child will make fewer mistakes and work more quickly. It allows the child to be more familiar with the question types and to develop a better exam technique. If passing is important then be prepared to make a major commitment in terms of the amount of time you spend with your child helping him or her to prepare.

To do well your child should arrive very well prepared. He or she should be fully aware of what the test involves, the type of questions it comprises and how long it lasts. Your child should be used to attempting the number of questions in the given time and so should avoid spending too long on some questions, risking being told that he or she has run out of time before finishing the test.

Organize the time you have for practice in two ways. First, work on questions with your child in a relaxed, quiet situation without time constraint or interruption. Check the answer to each question as you go along. Congratulate your child on the questions he or she got right, go over any questions to which the answer was wrong and try to help the child understand where he or she went wrong. Practise on more questions of that type and congratulate your child when he or she masters some-thing previously found difficult.

Keep practising this way until your child can confidently answer most types of question to be faced in the real exam. Undertake this kind of practice frequently but always be prepared to stop on any occasion that your child becomes tired or if the experience becomes unenjoyable. Little and often is the best approach.

Once your child is ready, start introducing practice tests where he or she has to answer questions against a time constraint and under exam-type conditions. Each chapter of questions includes a mock test with a suggested time limit. Use these questions to create a realistic practice test so that your child can get used to answering questions under the pressure of time and can build up speed and confidence under exam-type conditions. Make up more practice tests using other questions from the book as you need.

Encourage your child to keep going if there is a succession of difficult questions; the next section of the test may comprise different material for which your child is better prepared. Work to ensure that your child does not spend too long on any one question and develops a sense of the time allowed. If your child has time left then make sure he or she checks the answers until the time runs out. Explain to your child that doing well in a test is hard work and not simply a matter of intelligence. He or she should keep going until told to stop and afterwards feel tired as a result of the effort.

After each test go over the answers, congratulating the child when he or she is correct and explaining the answer to any that he or she got wrong. At all times keep the experience positive and constructive. If your child failed to attempt all the questions then remind him or her before the next test to speed up and encourage him or her along through that test.

There is no pass or fail of these practice tests and you should not draw any conclusions from your child's score. They are simply intended as an aid to learning.

Don't worry if you come across a question that you do not understand or cannot answer. It is common for parents to have to revise some forgotten skills or knowledge when helping their children with homework. Use the explanation when provided to help. Ask your child to explain the answer to you. Your child will enjoy working together this way.

What to expect on the day

If you have undertaken practice with your child then taking the real test should not present too anxious an occasion. The test format and question types should be entirely familiar.

Encourage your child simply to try his or her best and even to look forward to the opportunity to demonstrate how much he or she has benefited from the time spent with you in preparation.

The exam will be organized in a way very reminiscent of the exams that you faced at school. It is most likely to be a paper-and-pencil test (rather than taken on a computer terminal) and the format will be either multiple choice (where the child must choose from one of a number of suggested answers) or short answer (which requires answers to be written in an answer box).

The exam is likely to be held at the school to which your child has applied and you will receive a date on which you are requested to attend with your child for the exam. It is likely to be held in the hall of the school, and many other children will be present. The tables and chairs will be organized in the normal way for exams. Parents or guardians will be asked to wait in another part of the school.

The children will be expected to leave any bags or coats with the accompanying adult and to take one of the available seats. A teacher administrating the exam will explain the procedure. Each child will be provided with an answer sheet and pencil and test booklet. The children will not be allowed to open the test booklet until they are told. The exam may well comprise a number of papers and there will be a few example questions for each of the papers. An opportunity to ask questions will be given before the test begins.

After the test the school marks the papers. It is likely to await all the test results before making any decisions about to whom to offer places. Any pass mark or decision over which stream to place a child in is relative to the score of all the children who took the exam that year. You will be informed of the result of your application by post possibly many months after the test date.

If you find a mistake in this book then accept my apologies and please do not allow it to undermine you or your child's confidence in the value of practice. I have tried hard to keep errors out and hope that I have not missed too many. I would be glad to hear of any that you find, care of Kogan Page, in order that they may be removed at the next reprint.

2

Mathematics

Work to ensure that your child is both confident and accurate in answering the questions making up this chapter. By all means encourage your child to use a calculator to check an answer or to understand better how an answer is arrived at but otherwise practise at answering these questions without a calculator.

Both short answer and multiple choice questions are provided. Answers and many explanations are found on pages 185 to 198.

At school your child may have been taught a method of answering a question different to the method you were taught. He or she may also have been encouraged to adopt one of a number of methods, depending on the particular sum. Ask your child to explain the method taught at school and wherever possible adopt that method.

It may be that your child can skip some sections of this chapter if you know that he or she is already well practised at the particular operations.

If your child finds the question difficult then do explain that the real test will contain questions that are difficult and that even the best-prepared candidate will get questions wrong. Be patient and practise mastering difficult questions with your child. When your child has made progress, review some earlier work and discuss with the child how much he or she has improved.

If it is some years since you did such maths and you are a little rusty then explain this to your child, refer to the many explanations provided and work to build up your speed and confidence together.

The chapter begins with a 26-question 'work quickly' test in which the child is allowed only five seconds for each question. This type of test will help develop a winning exam technique by helping your child realize just how quickly you have to work to do well in a test. It will also help your child to learn to avoid wasting time on difficult questions by skipping them and using the time available to answer questions he or she finds more straightforward. If you find this quick test useful then make up more examples.

At the end of the chapter you will find a 20-question real-life problems practice test. If you want to practise on more tests then select a variety of other questions from this chapter and allow one minute a question (feel free to adjust the time allowed to suit your child's situation).

A quick test!

Only five seconds a question allowed.

Find a quiet, comfortable place where you will not be interrupted and using a stopwatch (many mobile phones have such a feature) or watch with a second hand prepare your child for the quick test.

Your child will need a pencil to write down the answers but do not use a calculator.

Go over the two practice questions and explain the answers.

Practice questions

1.   8 + 5 = ?

Answer ☐

Answer 13.

2.   How many vowels does the word 'spelling' contain?

Answer ☐

Answer 2 (the 'e' and the 'i').

Allow your child 2 minutes 10 seconds to attempt the 26 questions that begin over the page.

Make sure that your child turns over the pages until he or she reaches the end of the test.

Encourage your child to work quickly and to keep going.

Make it fun.

Do not turn over the page until you are ready to begin.

Q1. 5 + 6 = ?

Answer ☐

Q2. 11 + 3 = ?

Answer ☐

Q3. Which month comes after August?

Answer ☐

Q4. What day of the week is before Tuesday?

Answer ☐

Q5. 15 – 9 = ?

Answer ☐

Q6. 30 – 15 =

Answer ☐

Q7. What is half of 36?

Answer ☐

Q8. 3 × 5 = ?

Answer ☐

Q9. 4 × 4 = ?

Answer ☐

Q10. How many days are there in January?

Answer ☐

Q11. What was the year five years before 1997?

Answer ☐

Q12. $3 \times 6 = ?$

Answer ☐

Q13. At what temperature in degrees centigrade does water boil?

Answer ☐

Q14. $40 \div 2 = ?$

Answer ☐

Q15. If it is 2 o'clock now what will the time be in 1 hour 45 minutes?

Answer ☐

Q16. How many vowels are there in the word 'nursemaid'?

Answer ☐

Q17. How many grams are there in half a kilogram?

Answer ☐

Q18. If the time is twelve fifteen, what will the time be in 20 minutes?

Answer

Q19. $23 - 5 + 2 = ?$

Answer

Q20. What day of the week is three days after Wednesday?

Answer

Q21. 3 centimetres is equal to how many millimetres?

Answer

Q22. $17 + 4 - 6 = ?$

Answer

Q23. What is half of 1 hour 30 minutes?

Answer

Q24. $3 - 2 + 7 = ?$

Answer

Q25. How many vowels are there in the word 'DOLPHIN'?

Answer

Q26.   What word is a verb?

Sing a song someone.

Answer

STOP; this is the end of the quick test.

Lots of essential practice maths questions

Feel free to skip some sections of this chapter if you know that your child is already well practised at the particular operations, or reorganize the material into more practice tests.

Add these without a calculator:

Q1.   270
       + 29

                                                    Answer [ ]

Q2.   46
       +142

                                                    Answer [ ]

Q3.   301
       +46

                                                    Answer [ ]

Q4.   432
       +257

                                                    Answer [ ]

Q5.   397
       +30

                                                    Answer [ ]

Q6.   88
       +106

                                                    Answer [ ]

Q7.   267
       +398

                                              Answer ☐

Q8.   999
       +101

                                              Answer ☐

Q9.   5,193
       +907

                                              Answer ☐

Q10.   6,009
       +6,791

                                              Answer ☐

Subtract these sums using only your brain and a pencil!

Q11.   658
       −134

                                              Answer ☐

Q12.   473
       −260

                                              Answer ☐

Q13.   596
       −505

                                              Answer ☐

Q14.   987
       −380

                                              Answer ☐

Q15.   345
         −250

                                                  Answer ☐

Q16.   733
         −305

                                                  Answer ☐

Q17.   408
         −139

                                                  Answer ☐

Q18.   638
         −289

                                                  Answer ☐

Q19.   916
         −737

                                                  Answer ☐

Q20.   800
         −178

                                                  Answer ☐

Multiply or divide these sums in your head:

Q21. 9 × 3 =

                                                  Answer ☐

Q22. 5 × 6 =

                                                  Answer ☐

Q23. $7 \times 7 =$

Answer ☐

Q24. $11 \times 4 =$

Answer ☐

Q25. $52 \times 4 =$

Answer ☐

Q26. $24 \times 3 =$

Answer ☐

Q27. $84 \div 2 =$

Answer ☐

Q28. $60 \div 5 =$

Answer ☐

Q29. $48 \div 6 =$

Answer ☐

Q30. $72 \div 12 =$

Answer ☐

Q31. Match 31,386 to how it is written in words:

A   Three hundred and one thousand, three hundred and eighty-six

B   Thirty-one thousand, three hundred and eighty-six

C   Three hundred and thirteen thousand, three hundred and eighty-six

D   Three hundred and thirteen thousand and eighty-six

Answer

Q32. What is 500 MORE than 325?

A   825

B   385

C   525

D   578

Answer

Q33. What is 500 LESS than 1,463?

A   836

B   953

C   963

D   1,963

Answer

Q34. What is 500 MORE than 20,696?

A   20,196

B   21,196

C   20,746

D   21,746

Answer

Q35. What is 2,101 MORE than 56?

A   2,560

B   7,600

C   2,157

D   2,011

Answer ☐

Q36. What is 128 MORE than 976?

A   1,004

B   1,104

C   1,114

D   848

Answer ☐

Q37. What is 2,004 LESS than 10,003?

A   7,999

B   8,001

C   799

D   12,007

Answer ☐

Q38. What is the highest place value in the number 105,302?

A   Hundred thousands

B   Ten thousands

C   Tens

D   Hundreds

Answer ☐

Q39.   What is the lowest place value in the number 983.5?

A   Hundreds

B   Ones

C   Tenths

D   Hundredths

Answer

Q40.   Write in the box the highest and lowest place value of 4,637.04.

Answer

| Highest |
| Lowest |

Q41.   Match the sum to the answer.

Sum:		Answer:	
A	100 ÷ 10	1	10
B	100 × 10	2	100
C	1,000 ÷ 100	3	1,000
D	100 × 100	4	10,000

Answer

| A |
| B |
| C |
| D |

Q42.   Divide 334 by 100.

A   0.0334

B   0.334

C   33.4

D   3.34

Answer

Q43. Divide 23,496 by 1,000.

A   2.3496

B   23.496

C   234.96

D   2,349.6

Answer ☐

Q44. Put these numbers into ascending order:

A   41,208

B   695.3

C   7,650

D   87,532

Answer ☐

Q45. Put these numbers into descending order:

A   0.975

B   0.275

C   0.786

D   3.004

Answer ☐

Q46. Divide 0.045 by 100.

A   0.045

B   4.5

C   0.0045

D   0.00045

Answer ☐

Q47. Multiply 0.932 by 100.

A   932.0

B   93.2

C   9.32

D   0.932

Answer

Q48. Put the temperatures into ascending order:

A   0

B   7

C   –3

D   11

E   3

F   –7

Answer

Q49. Work out –3 + –3 =

A   6

B   0

C   –9

D   –6

Answer

Q50. Work out –2 – –2.

A   4

B   –4

C   0

Answer ☐

Q51. Work out –1 + 9.

A   8

B   –8

C   10

D   –10

Answer ☐

Q52. Work out –7 – 5.

A   2

B   12

C   –2

D   –12

Answer ☐

Q53. Work out –6 + 6.

A   6

B   –6

C   0

Answer ☐

Q54. Work out −14 − 3.

A   17

B   −17

C   −11

D   11

Answer

Q55. Work out 10 − −8.

A   −18

B   18

C   0

D   −2

Answer

Q56. What number does the arrow point to?

A   8.5

B   8.75

C   9.75

D   11

Answer

Q57. What number does the arrow point to?

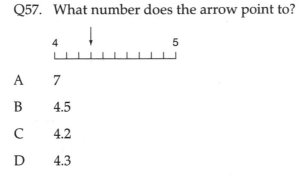

A   7

B   4.5

C   4.2

D   4.3

Answer

Q58. What number does the arrow point to?

A   0.24

B   0.6

C   0.25

D   2.4

Answer

Q59. What equivalent fraction does 3/9 cancel to?

A   1/4

B   1/3

C   2/3

D   1/2

Answer

Q60. What equivalent fraction does 8/12 cancel to?

A   1/4

B   1/3

C   2/3

D   1/2

Answer ☐

Q61. What equivalent fraction does 25/40 cancel to?

A   9/10

B   6/12

C   4/16

D   5/8

Answer ☐

Q62. What is 1/6 of £4.80?

A   £1.20

B   96p

C   80p

D   £1.60

Answer ☐

Q63. What is 2/5 of 10 meters^2?

A   2m^2

B   5m^2

C   1m^2

D   4m^2

Answer ☐

Q64. What is 1/9 of 63km?

A   7km

B   5km

C   6.3km

D   8km

Answer

Q65. What is 4/5 of 50 minutes?

A   10 minutes

B   30 minutes

C   40 minutes

D   20 minutes

Answer

Q66. What is 7/12 of 60 minutes?

A   5 minutes

B   35 minutes

C   30 minutes

D   45 minutes

Answer

Q67. If 6/8 is equivalent to ?/32, what is the value of the unknown numerator?

A   12

B   16

C   18

D   24

Answer

Q68. If 2/9 is equivalent to 12/?, what is the value of the unknown denominator?

A   54

B   18

C   27

D   63

Answer

Q69. Which is the smallest?

A   0.2

B   1/2

C   1/4

D   1/3

E   0.125

Answer

Q70. Which is the smallest?

A   0.2

B   2/8

C   0.25

D   3/18

Answer

Q71. What is the smallest?

A   0.125

B   12/16

C   1/6

D   0.33

Answer

Q72. Which is the largest?

A   1/7

B   0.3

C   1/8

D   3/12

Answer ☐

Q73. Which is the largest?

A   1/2

B   0.4

C   2/5

D   6/21

Answer ☐

Q74. Change 0.44 into a percentage.

A   4.4%

B   22%

C   44%

D   0.44%

Answer ☐

Q75. Change 0.01 into a percentage.

A   10%

B   100%

C   1%

D   5%

Answer ☐

Q76. Change 25% into a fraction.

A   1/5

B   1/3

C   1/4

D   1/2

Answer

Q77. Change 3/10 into a percentage.

A   3.33%

B   30%

C   10%

D   3%

Answer

Q78. Change 5/20 into a percentage.

A   20%

B   5%

C   25%

D   50%

Answer

Q79. Change 70% into a decimal.

A   0.7

B   7

C   0.07

D   1.42

Answer

Q80. Change 45% into a decimal.

A   4.5

B   4.05

C   45

D   0.45

Answer

Q81. Which is the smallest?

A   12.5%

B   1/7

C   0.5

Answer

Q82. Which is the largest?

A   63%

B   3/5

C   0.83

Answer

Q83. Which number is closest to 1?

A   0.01

B   0.12

C   0.91

D   0.56

Answer

Q84. Which number is closest to 1?

A   1.08

B   1.11

C   0.80

D   0.69

E   1.41

Answer

Q85. What is 476.73 expressed to 1 decimal point?

A   477

B   476

C   476.7

D   476.8

Answer

Q86. What is 2.079 expressed to 2 decimal points?

A   2.10

B   2.08

C   2.07

D   2.06

E   2.09

Answer

Q87. What number can you multiply by itself to get 25?

A   4

B   2

C   6

D   3

E   5

Answer

Q88. What number can you add to itself to get 24?

A   6

B   3

C   9

D   12

Answer

Q89. What number do you multiply by itself to get 36?

A   2

B   3

C   4

D   5

E   6

Answer

Q90. What number do you start with if you multiply it by itself and then multiply the answer by 4 to get 36?

A   1

B   2

C   3

D   4

Answer

Q91. What number do you start with if you multiply it by itself and then multiply the answer by 5 to get 20?

A   1

B   2

C   3

D   4

Answer

Q92. Which of the suggested answers has two numbers that are both multiples of 4?

A   16, 18, 12

B   7, 11, 13

C   21, 22, 24

D   6, 7, 8

Answer

Q93. Which of the suggested numbers contain two numbers that are both multiples of 6?

A   9, 8, 6

B   12, 11, 14

C   36, 20, 24

D   62, 64, 60

E   16, 22, 18

Answer ▢

Q94. Which of the suggested answers contains a number that is a multiple of 3, 4 and 6?

A   21, 18, 20

B   16, 8, 33

C   6, 10, 19

D   13, 36, 23

E   30, 8, 15

Answer ▢

Q95. Which list contains a number that is a multiple of 6, 8 and 12?

A   36, 32

B   40, 30

C   52, 16

D   56, 48

E   21, 35

Answer ▢

Q96.   What number do you get if you divide 72 by 8?

A   6

B   7

C   8

D   9

Answer

Q97.   What number do you get if you divide 66 by 6?

A   9

B   10

C   11

D   12

Answer

Q98.   What number do you get if you divide 84 by 7?

A   12

B   13

C   14

D   15

Answer

Q99.   If you divide 77 by 11 you get the number:

A   5

B   6

C   7

D   8

Answer

Q100. If you divide 40 by 5 and then multiply the answer by 3, what number do you get?

A   8

B   16

C   24

D   48

Answer

Q101. What number do you get if you divide 18 by 6 and then multiply the answer by 4?

A   9

B   12

C   18

D   24

Answer

Q102. What number do you get if you multiply 12 by 5 and then divide the answer by 10?

A   6

B   30

C   10

D   5

Answer

Q103. Which of the following numbers can you divide exactly by 9?

A   64

B   54

C   74

D   84

Answer

Q104. Which number can you divide exactly by 7?

A   93

B   81

C   102

D   77

Answer

Q105. Which number can you divide exactly by 8?

A   72

B   49

C   63

D   54

Answer

Q106. Which one of the following numbers can you divide exactly by 6?

A   65

B   32

C   43

D   54

Answer

Q107. Which number can you divide exactly by both 6 and 9?

A   42

B   30

C   36

D   45

Answer

Q108. Which of the following pair of numbers can be divided exactly by both 4 and 3?

A   16, 60

B   15, 90

C   12, 48

D   36, 100

Answer ☐

Q109. What number do you start with if you multiply it by 3 and then double it and get the answer 30?

A   15

B   5

C   10

D   2

Answer ☐

Q110. What number do you start with if you multiply it by 5, then double it and get the answer 100?

A   1

B   15

C   5

D   10

Answer ☐

Q111. What number do you start with if you multiply it by 4, then double it and then divide it by 12 to get the figure 4?

A   6

B   7

C   8

D   9

Answer

Q112. What number do you start with if you multiply it by 6, then double it and then divide it by 12 to get the figure 10?

A   6

B   12

C   7

D   10

Answer

Q113. What number do you start with if you divide it by 4, halve it and then multiply it by 5 to get the figure 20?

A   8

B   16

C   32

D   9

Answer

Q114. What number do you start with if you halve it, multiply it by 7 and then divide it by 6 to get the figure 7?

A   7

B   12

C   9

D   6

Answer ☐

Q115. What number do you start with if you halve it, then divide it by 4 and then multiply it by 6 to get 12?

A   16

B   18

C   20

D   22

Answer ☐

Q116. What number do you start with if you multiply it by 10, then divide it by 3 and then halve it to get the figure 20?

A   6

B   9

C   10

D   12

Answer ☐

Q117. Which number completes the following sequence?

1, 6, 11, 16, ?

A   19

B   20

C   21

D   22

Answer

Q118. Which number completes the following sequence?

10, 13, 16, 19, ?

A   21

B   22

C   23

D   24

Answer

Q119. Which of the suggested numbers completes this sequence?

110, 122, 134, 146, ?

A   155

B   156

C   157

D   158

Answer

Q120. What number completes the sequence?

2, 4, 8, ?

A   10

B   12

C   16

D   24

Answer

Q121. What number completes this sequence?

4, 12, ?, 108

A   35

B   36

C   37

D   38

Answer

Q122. What number completes this sequence?

?, 20, 40, 80, 160

A   1

B   2

C   5

D   10

Answer

Q123. Complete the following sequence:

10, 100, 1,000, 10,000

A   100,000

B   1,000,000

C   12,000

D   10,000,000

Answer

Q124. What number completes this sequence?

1, 2, ?, 8, 16

A   3

B   4

C   5

D   6

Answer

Q125. Complete this sequence:

400, 200, ?, 50, 25

A   100

B   75

C   125

D   150

Answer

Q126. Complete this sequence:

24, ?, 36, 42, 48

A   26

B   28

C   30

D   32

Answer

Q127. What number completes this sequence?

?, 10, 3, –4

A   17

B   13

C   14

D   12

Answer

Q128. Complete this sequence:

120, 80, 40, 0, ?

A   –10

B   –80

C   –20

D   –40

Answer

Q129. What suggested answer completes this sequence?

?, 54, 63, 72

A   36

B   45

C   27

D   18

Answer

Q130. What number completes the following sequence?

90, 75, ?, 45

A   50

B   55

C   60

D   65

Answer

Q131. Which suggested answer correctly identifies the following sequence?

1, 8, 27, 64, 125

A   The sequence of square numbers

B   The sequence of cube numbers

C   The sequence of prime numbers

Answer

Q132. Which suggested answer correctly identifies the following sequence?

2, 3, 5, 7, 11, 13, 17

A   The sequence of square numbers

B   The sequence of cube numbers

C   The sequence of prime numbers

Answer ☐

Q133. Which suggested answer correctly identifies the following sequence?

1, 4, 9, 16, 25

A   The sequence of square numbers

B   The sequence of cube numbers

C   The sequence of prime numbers

Answer ☐

Q134. At the school assembly Ella saw that there were 18 rows of children with 14 children sitting in each row. How many children were at the assembly?

A   238

B   252

C   266

D   234

Answer ☐

Q135. If 25 pieces of paper were numbered 1–15 and folded so the numbers could not be seen and placed in a bag what is the probability of choosing a number more than 12?

A   4/15

B   1/5

C   Even

D   2/5

Answer

Q136. Orlando was helping his dad to buy food for his birthday party. They decided to buy cheese sticks. If each packet contains 4 sticks and Orlando had invited 14 children to his party, how many packets did they need to buy in order that each child could have a cheese stick?

A   3

B   4

C   5

D   6

Answer

Q137. Two friends decided to sell some of their toys. They raised 80p for a Power Ranger sword, £1.15 for a collection of Barbie dolls and 55p for a teddy bear. They divided all the money they received equally between them. How much did each friend receive?

A   £2.40

B   £1.25

C   £1.15

D   £2.35

Answer

Q138. If you choose a number from the list 2, 3, 4, 5, what is the probability of you choosing an even number?

A   An even chance

B   A less than even chance

C   A more than even chance

Answer ☐

Q139. On a school trip to a zoo each child was asked to bring 95p as a contribution towards the cost of the trip. If £19 was collected, how many children paid to go on the trip?

A   18

B   19

C   20

D   21

Answer ☐

Q140. A pack of stickers costs 73 pence. How much will 6 packs cost?

A   £4.38

B   £4.28

C   £4.22

D   £4.32

Answer ☐

Q141. In a school vote the following results were obtained:

Yes   185
No   220
Undecided   ?
Total   550

What is the missing number?

A   35

B   330

C   405

D   145

Answer

Q142. 300 people entered a fun run and 4/5ths finished the run in under two hours. How many people is this?

A   60

B   240

C   120

D   180

Answer

Q143. A shop sells 2 chocolate-flavoured ice creams for every 1 mint-flavoured one. If a total of 180 ice creams are sold on a sunny day, how many would be chocolate flavoured?

A   60

B   180

C   120

D   90

Answer

Q144. Joy's sister makes and sells jewellery. The cost of materials represents 30% of the sale price. If she takes £270 in sales what will be the cost of materials?

A   £81

B   £8.10

C   £189

D   £18.90

Answer

Q145. The pie chart and key illustrate the percentages of time that types of dolphin were sighted in the sea around the UK.

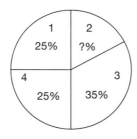

Key
1. Striped dolphin
2. Common dolphin
3. Bottlenose dolphin
4. Spotted dolphin

If spotted dolphins were sighted 30 times how many times were common dolphins sighted?

A   30

B   42

C   18

D   15

Answer

Q146. If the fire-fighters went into a smoke-filled building at 12.17 and came out at 1.53, for how long were they in the building?

A   70 minutes

B   96 minutes

C   43 minutes

D   53 minutes

Answer

Q147. In a pack of mixed nuts the following number of each type were found:

Brazil   40
Almond   30
Pecan   20
Hazelnut   ?
Walnut   15

If the mean was 25, how many hazelnuts were there in the packet?

A   15

B   25

C   30

D   20

Answer

Q148. If the ferry takes 20 minutes to cross from the Isle of Wight to Portsmouth and the train takes 1 hour 20 minutes to reach London Waterloo, what fraction of the whole journey time is spent on the ferry?

A   1/8

B   1/6

C   1/5

D   1/12

Answer

Q149. Carlo was 4 when his cousin was 11. How old will Carlo be when his cousin finishes university at the age of 23 years?

A   13

B   14

C   15

D   16

Answer

Q150. If Mexico City is 6 hours behind the UK and the time in the UK is 14.00 what is the time in Mexico City?

A   6.00

B   7.00

C   8.00

D   9.00

Answer

Q151. If the average family takes 30 taxi rides a year, while a family with someone with a disability takes 40% more taxi rides, how many rides each year does a family with a disabled member take?

A   34

B   18

C   42

D   12

Answer

Q152. If a bag contains 2 white, 3 black and 1 green disc and you pick a disc from the bag with your eyes closed, what is the probability of you picking the green disc?

A   Even

B   1/3

C   1/4

D   1/6

Answer

Q153. Find the mean of the following numbers:

25, 30, 20, 22, 13

A   19

B   20

C   21

D   22

Answer

Q154. If your sister was given the following coins, how much money would she have?

2 × £2	1 × £1	3 × 50p
2 × 20p	4 × 2p	7 × 1p

A   £7.05

B   £7.07

C   £6.98

D   £6.50

Answer

Q155. If you bought six birthday cards, all identically priced, and paid with a £5 note and received £1.16 in change, how much was each card?

A   64p

B   65p

C   £1.16

D   £3.84

Answer

Q156. If a farmer has 735 oranges to send to market and she sends them in crates each of which holds 58 oranges, how many crates will the farmer need?

A   11

B   12

C   13

D   14

Answer

Q157. In 2001 over 600 people visited a museum; in 2002 that figure doubled and in 2003 the figure doubled again. How many people visited the museum in 2003?

A   Over 1,800 but less than 2,400

B   Over 2,400

C   Less than 1,800

D   2,400 exactly

Answer

Q158. A survey found that 360 children wanted the blue team to win while 120 supported the red team. What was the ratio between the blue and red team supporters?

A   2:1

B   1:3

C   5:1

D   3:1

Answer

Q159. If 9 out of 12 singers in a choir had sore throats, what percentage of singers were suffering this painful condition?

A   25%

B   50%

C   75%

D   60%

Answer

Q160. £100 is to be divided between two children in the ratio of 3:2. How much is each child to receive?

A   £30 and £20

B   £70 and £30

C   £80 and £20

D   £60 and £40

Answer

Q161. In a class of 33 children, 2 forgot their game kit. Which of the suggested percentages is the closest estimate of the percentage who forgot their kit?

A   2%

B   16%

C   6%

D   8%

Answer

Q162. In a survey of 165 people, two-thirds said that they watched a TV programme. The rest said that they did not watch it. How many said that they did not watch the programme?

A   65

B   110

C   55

D   33

Answer

Q163. If you roll a dice and toss a coin what is the chance of getting a six and heads?

A   1 in 12 and even

B   1 in 6 and even

C   1 in 6 and 1 in 3

D   1 in 3 and 1 in 3

Answer ☐

Practice real-life problems test

This test contains 20 questions. Allow your child either 35 or 40 minutes to attempt them (depending on your assessment of how easy he or she finds these sorts of questions).

Use this practice test to develop your child's test technique. In particular, encourage your child to do the following:

- Work quickly and do not spend too long on any one question. The test deliberately starts with more difficult questions for this reason.

- Do any working out on a separate piece of paper.

- Practise estimating and rounding sums to more convenient amounts.

- Keep going even if you cannot answer a series of questions as you may be able to answer later questions.

Once your child has completed the test go over the answers and explanations together taking care to compliment your child when he or she has got answers right. There is not a pass or fail mark; simply use the result to identify where more practice is needed. Focus future work on any types of question that your child finds difficult and if necessary practise to build up confidence and speed in multiplication or division.

Do not turn the page until you are ready to begin.

Q1. If a popular drink is made of water, apple juice and blackcurrant juice to the ratio 7:2:1, how much blackcurrant juice is found in a 200ml bottle?

A   10ml

B   20ml

C   40ml

D   30ml

Answer

Q2. The pie chart and key illustrate what 25 children did when they finished school at 16 years of age.

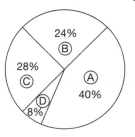

Key
A Stayed on for sixth form at their school
B Did a vocational training course
C Went to a sixth form college
D Got a job

Which sum will allow you to work out the number of children who got a job or did a vocational training course?

A   64% of 25

B   28% of 25

C   32% of 25

D   8% of 25

Answer

Q3.   The table shows the number of votes received by each of four
       candidates for the position of school representative.

Candidate	Tom	Helen	Yunus	Ricky
Votes by boys	15	12	16	13
Votes by girls	17	19	15	16

Which candidate won the election?

A   Tom

B   Helen

C   Yunus

D   Ricky

Answer

Q4.   The bar chart illustrates the number of days it rained each month
       over five months.

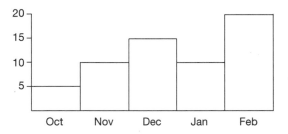

On how many more days did it rain in February than November?

A   20

B   15

C   10

D   5

Answer

Q5.   If you and three friends use a square spinner to decide who
       should eat the last sweet in the packet what are the chances that it
       will be you?

A   Even

B   0.25

C   0.2

D   1/3

                                                        Answer ☐ .

Q6.   For the first ride of the day on a merry-go-round, all 50 places
       were taken. For the next ride, 20 got off and 15 got on. For the
       third ride, 30 got off and 12 got on. How many free places were
       there at the start of the third ride?

A   27

B   15

C   45

D   23

                                                        Answer ☐

Q7.   Ali had read 73 pages of a book that contained 149 pages in total.
       How many more pages remained before he finished his book?

A   73

B   74

C   75

D   76

                                                        Answer ☐

Q8.   If a cable 1,280m long is formed into a square, how long will each side of the square be?

A   320m

B   220m

C   540m

D   640m

Answer

Q9.   If 25 girls and 15 boys went on a school trip, what fraction of the total were boys?

A   3/8

B   4/7

C   5/8

D   3/5

Answer

Q10.   Mum had to cut a pizza to share equally between 6 children, 4 girls and 2 boys. What share of the pizza did mum give to the boys?

A   1/2

B   1/4

C   1/5

D   1/3

Answer

Q11. If apples cost 60 pence a kilo and pears cost 25% more, how much will 2 kilos of pears cost?

A   75p

B   90p

C   £1.20

D   £1.50

Answer

Q12. Allegra gets £1.57 a month interest from her savings and £15 a week helping her dad in the family store. How much does she earn in a year?

A   £798.84

B   £788.84

C   £858.50

D   £780.00

Answer

Q13. Fay is to catch a flight to visit her grandparents. The flight leaves at 18.44 and she must check in 2 hours before departure. To get to the airport Fay must catch a train from Farlow station; the train journey takes 1 hour 17 minutes. Use the timetable provided to calculate which train Fay should catch.

Shawfield	13.12	14.54	15.42	16.15
Farlow	13.36	15.27	16.06	16.39
Fenwick	13.53	15.44	16.23	16.56
Portland	14.06	15.59	16.36	17.09
Airport	?	?	?	?

A   13.12

B   15.27

C   16.39

D   13.36

Answer

Q14. If the sun rises at 7.24 am and sets at 4.06 pm, how many hours of daylight will there be?

A   8 hours 36 minutes

B   8 hours 6 minutes

C   6 hours 32 minutes

D   8 hours 42 minutes

Answer

Q15. If you received £3.03 change from £15 when you bought three identical films, how much was each film?

A   £2.99

B   £3.00

C   £3.99

D   £2.75

Answer

Q16. To make a cappuccino requires 6gm of coffee. How many cups can you make from a 3kg catering pack of coffee?

A   1,000

B   250

C   500

D   750

Answer

Q17. If you spent £32.70 on cinema tickets and each ticket cost £5.45, how many tickets did you buy?

A   4

B   5

C   6

D   7

Answer

Q18. Use the conversion graph to identify which of the estimated conversions is incorrect.

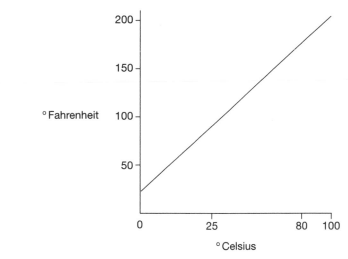

A $0°C = 32°F$

B $25°C = 57°F$

C $80°C = 175°F$

D $100°C = 212°F$

Answer

Q19. If you bought the listed items and paid with a £20 note, what change would you expect?

List
Pot of jam	£1.18
Bottle of squash	87p
Bottle of oil	68p
Bag of onions	58p
Newspaper	50p
Tube of toothpaste	£1.84

A   £13.60

B   £12.76

C   £14.35

D   £5.65

Answer

Q20. If the time now is 2.25 am what was the time 6 hours 30 minutes ago?

A   7.55 pm

B   8.55 pm

C   8.55 am

D   7.55 am

Answer

End of Test

3

Verbal reasoning

In this chapter, five styles of question are covered. A series of warm-up questions are provided and the chapter concludes with a 25-question practice test.

You may wish to skip the warm-up questions if your child would find them easy, or some of the styles of question if they are not relevant to the test faced by your child.

The main benefits of this practice are:

- to ensure that your child understands the demands of the question types;
- to build your child's vocabulary especially in the rather artificial situation where the word is isolated and lacks a context provided by a sentence or paragraph;
- to encourage your child to answer questions even when he or she does not know the meaning of all the words.

Be sure that your child understands that a great many children find these questions and these types of real test difficult and that getting questions wrong or not knowing the meanings is entirely normal. Practise lots, as it can lead to a marked improvement in performance in this type of test as the child gets used to the strangeness of the task and develops his or her vocabulary.

Answers are found on pages 199–206. Some explanations are given but meanings can be looked up.

It is really good practice to use a dictionary or thesaurus every time your child is unsure of what a word means. Take a trip to a bookshop with your child and choose a dictionary and thesaurus together. Have a look at the *Oxford Concise School Dictionary* and *Oxford Concise School Thesaurus* or the slightly more approachable *Oxford Children's Dictionary* and *Oxford Children's Thesaurus*. But let it be your child's choice.

Warm-up questions

Q1. What new word do you make if you remove
the 's' from 'skid'?

Answer

Q2. What new word do you make if you remove
the 't' from 'trip'?

Answer

Q3. What new word do you make if you remove
the 'u' from 'cause'?

Answer

Q4. Which letter can you remove from each of the following words to
make two new words:

neat, hoarse

Answer

Q5. What new word do you get if you remove the
'n' in 'hunt'?

Answer

Q6. Which letter can you remove from these two words to make two
new words?

clock, chip

Answer

Q7. Which letter can you remove from these two words to make two
new words?

find, tend

Answer

Q8. What letter can you move from 'shed' and 'skid' to make two new words?

Answer ☐

Q9. What two new words do you make if you remove a letter from 'dream' and 'danger'?

Answer ▭

Q10. What two words do you make if you remove the 'e' from 'mean' and 'meat'?

Answer ▭

Q11. What letter can you move from 'glow' and 'dog' to make two new words?

Answer ☐

Q12. What letter can you move from 'shame' and 'shake' to make two new words?

Answer ☐

Q13. What two new words can you make if you remove a letter from 'claim' and 'vain'?

Answer ▭

Q14. What two new words can you make if you remove a letter from 'think' and 'tank'?

Answer ▭

Q15. What letter can you move from 'warm' and 'wash' to make two new words?

Answer ☐

Q16. What letter can you move from 'smell' and 'seem' to make two new words?

Answer

Q17. What two new words can you make if you remove a letter from 'grave' and 'grope'?

Answer

Q18. What letter can you move from 'plain' and 'place' to make two new words?

Answer

Q19. What two new words do you make if you remove a letter from 'cheap' and 'chunk'?

Answer

Q20. What two new words do you make if you remove a letter from 'draw' and 'mend'?

Answer

Q21. What letter can you move from 'stage' and 'site' to make two new words?

Answer

Q22. What two new words do you make if you remove a letter from 'hair' and 'harm'?

Answer

Q23. What letter can you move from 'form' and 'farm' to make two new words?

Answer

Q24. What two new words do you make if you remove a letter from 'cold' and 'clog'?

Answer

Q25. What two new words do you make if you remove a letter from 'dear' and 'drip'?

Answer

Q26. What letter can you move from 'fade' and 'dead' to make two new words?

Answer

Q27. What letter can you move from 'grumble' and 'gruff' to make two new words?

Answer

Q28. What letter can you move from 'flower' and 'flow' to make two new words?

Answer

Q29. What letter can you move from 'sign' and 'ghost' to make two new words?

Answer

Q30. What two new words can you make by removing a letter from 'chart' and 'chase'?

Answer

Q31. What letter can you move from 'pale' and 'paste' to make two new words?

Answer

Q32. What letter can you move from 'wind' and 'kind' to make two new words?

Answer

Q33. What two new words can you make if you remove a letter from 'cheat' and 'crack'?

Answer

Q34. What letter can you move from 'play' and 'plan' to make two new words?

Answer

Q35. What letter can you move from 'main' and 'pain' to make two new words?

Answer

Q36. What two new words can you make if you remove a letter from 'plot' and 'plant'?

Answer

Question type 1

Your task is to move a letter from the first word and put it into the second word to create two new words. When you have worked out which letter it is and what two new words you make, record your answer in the answer box. Sometimes the question requires you to record the letter that you move; other times your task is to write in the answer box the new words that you have created.

For example:

Q37. Which letter can you move from 'hate' and put in 'not' to make two new words?

Answer [e]

Answer: move the 'e' to make 'hat' and 'note'.

Alternatively:

Q38. Which two new words do you create by moving a letter from 'acorn' and putting it in 'cute'?

Answer [**corn and acute**]

You find the answer by moving the letter 'a' to make 'corn' and 'acute'.

Try these further examples:

Q39. Which letter can you move from 'land' and put in 'earn' to make two new words?

Answer [ ]

Q40. Which two new words do you create if you move a letter from 'lead' and put it in 'men'?

Answer [ ]

Q41. Which letter can you move from 'main' and put in 'host' to make two new words?

Answer

Q42. Which two new words do you create if you move one letter from 'made' and put it in 'star'?

Answer

Q43. Which letter can you move from 'burst' and put in 'tick' to make two new words?

Answer

Q44. Which letter can you move from 'card' and put in 'gran' to make two new words?

Answer

Q45. Which two new words do you create if you move a letter from 'faint' and put it in 'art'?

Answer

Q46. Which letter can you move from 'noisy' and put in 'char' to make two new words?

Answer

Q47. Which two new words do you create if you move a letter from 'loose' and put it in 'stop'?

Answer

Q48. Which letter can you move from 'hurt' and put in 'pot' to make two new words?

Answer

Q49. Which two new words do you create if you move a letter from 'crease' and put it in 'had'?

Answer

Q50. Which letter can you move from 'prove' and put in 'rod' to make two new words?

Answer

Q51. Which two new words do you make if you move a letter from 'cover' and put it in 'lean'?

Answer

Q52. Which letter can you move from 'snip' and put in 'cure' to make two new words?

Answer

Q53. Which letter can you move from 'friend' and put in 'chat' to make two new words?

Answer

Q54. Which letter can you move from 'small' and put in 'kip' to make two new words?

Answer

Q55. Which two new words do you make if you move a letter from 'gasp' and put it in 'mile'?

Answer

Q56. Which letter can you move from 'pierce' and put in 'dive' to make two new words?

Answer

Q57. Which two new words do you make if you move a letter from 'write' and put it in 'ant'?

Answer

Q58. Which letter can you move from 'skin' and put in 'oil' to make two new words?

Answer

Q59. Which letter can you move from 'lucky' and put in 'silk' to make two new words?

Answer

Q60. Which letter can you move from 'heart' and put in 'hash' to make two new words?

Answer

Q61. Which two new words do you make if you move a letter from 'space' and put it in 'harp'?

Answer

Q62. Which two new words do you make if you move a letter from 'deny' and put it in 'dirt'?

Answer

Q63. Which two new words do you make if you move a letter from 'pant' and put it in 'join'?

Answer

Q64. Which two new words do you make if you move a letter from 'skill' and put it in 'lip'?

Answer

Q65. Which letter can you move from 'stick' and put in 'seal' to make two new words?

Answer

Q66. Which letter can you move from 'post' and put in 'pray' to make two new words?

Answer

Q67. Which letter can you move from 'slot' and put in 'our' to make two new words?

Answer

Q68. Which two new words can you make if you move a letter from 'beet' and put it in 'but'?

Answer

Q69. Which two new words do you make if you move a letter from 'plant' and put it in 'read'?

Answer

Question type 2

Your task is to find a four-letter word that is made up of the end of one word and the beginning of the next.

For example:

Q70. Find a four-letter word made up of the end of one word and the beginning of the next:

takeoff, logical, alien

Answer | **flog** |

The answer is 'flog'.

Helpful tip: Do not be put off if a word starts with a capital letter. It can still be included as part of the new word.

Now try these examples:

Q71. Find a four-letter word made up of the end of one word and the beginning of the next:

blaze, referee, flight

Answer | |

Q72. Find a four-letter word made up of the end of one word and the beginning of the next:

class, public, lipstick

Answer | |

Q73. Find a four-letter word made up of the end of one word and the beginning of the next:

negative, illusion, slow

Answer | |

Q74. Find a four-letter word made up of the end of one word and the beginning of the next:

Neptune, editor, impossible

Answer

Q75. Find a four-letter word made up of the end of one word and the beginning of the next:

recluse, education, launch

Answer

Q76. Find a four-letter word made up of the end of one word and the beginning of the next:

harsh, staff, lopsided

Answer

Q77. Find a four-letter word made up of the end of one word and the beginning of the next:

harmony, massacre, adequate

Answer

Q78. Find a four-letter word made up of the end of one word and the beginning of the next:

rinse, dynamic, loggerhead

Answer

Q79. Find a four-letter word made up of the end of one word and the beginning of the next:

recipe, allotment, language

Answer

Q80. Find a four-letter word made up of the end of one word and the beginning of the next:

microchip, lottery, naughty

Answer

Q81. Find a four-letter word made up of the end of one word and the beginning of the next:

awesome, Atlantic, eligible

Answer

Q82. Find two four-letter words made up of the end of one word and the beginning of the next:

cross, panorama, lettuce

Answer

Q83. Find a four-letter word made up of the end of one word and the beginning of the next:

theft, negotiate, aromatic

Answer

Q84. Find a four-letter word made up of the end of one word and the beginning of the next:

maximal, society, ugly

Answer

Q85. Find a four-letter word made up of the end of one word and the beginning of the next:

marshmallow, escape, slouch

Answer

Q86. Find a four-letter word made up of the end of one word and the beginning of the next:

contrast, gallop, layer

Answer

Q87. Find a four-letter word made up of the end of one word and the beginning of the next:

worship, masculine, education

Answer

Q88. Find a four-letter word made up of the end of one word and the beginning of the next:

slither, marmalade, allergy

Answer

Q89. Find a four-letter word made up of the end of one word and the beginning of the next:

pup, leader, ebb

Answer

Q90. Find a four-letter word made up of the end of one word and the beginning of the next:

annoy, manifesto, practice

Answer

Q91. Find a four-letter word made up of the end of one word and the beginning of the next:

repair, contravene, atmosphere

Answer

Q92. Find a four-letter word made up of the end of one word and the beginning of the next:

jealous, contrast, episode

Answer [ ]

Q93. Find a four-letter word made up of the end of one word and the beginning of the next:

welcome, guarantee, muddle

Answer [ ]

Q94. Find a four-letter word made up of the end of one word and the beginning of the next:

school, exhale, approve

Answer [ ]

Q95. Find a four-letter word made up of the end of one word and the beginning of the next:

roughly, guinea, repair

Answer [ ]

Q96. Find a four-letter word made up of the end of one word and the beginning of the next:

explode, episode, eerie

Answer [ ]

Q97. Find a four-letter word made up of the end of one word and the beginning of the next:

hardware, annoy, magic

Answer [ ]

Q98.   Find a four-letter word made up of the end of one word and the beginning of the next:

inferno, sympathy, cabin

Answer

Q99.   Find a four-letter word made up of the end of one word and the beginning of the next:

order, hatch, opinion

Answer

Q100. Find a four-letter word made up of the end of one word and the beginning of the next:

virtue, brake, epoch

Answer

Q101. Find a four-letter word made up of the end of one word and the beginning of the next:

knowledge, homicide, adverse

Answer

Q102. Find a four-letter word made up of the end of one word and the beginning of the next:

fringe, manner, obedient

Answer

Q103. Find a four-letter word made up of the end of one word and the beginning of the next:

window, average, opponent

Answer

Q104. Find a four-letter word made up of the end of one word and the beginning of the next:

dwindle, socialism, ossify

Answer [   ]

Q105. Find three four-letter words made up of the end of one word and the beginning of the next:

zero, penalty, repeat

Answer [   ]

Q106. Find a four-letter word made up of the end of one word and the beginning of the next:

palmist, establish, shadow

Answer [   ]

Q107. Find a four-letter word made up of the end of one word and the beginning of the next:

padlock, ingenious, humour

Answer [   ]

Q108. Find a four-letter word made up of the end of one word and the beginning of the next:

dustcart, hunch, Ealing

Answer [   ]

Q109. Find a four-letter word made up of the end of one word and the beginning of the next:

tribe, statement, advice

Answer [   ]

Q110. Find a four-letter word made up of the end of one word and the beginning of the next:

difficult, through, average

Answer

Q111. Find two four-letter words made up of the end of one word and the beginning of the next:

overcast, ripen, suffer

Answer

Q112. Find a four-letter word made up of the end of one word and the beginning of the next:

dangle, incursive, stumble

Answer

Q113. Find a four-letter word made up of the end of one word and the beginning of the next:

idealistic, knowledgeable, people

Answer

Q114. Find a four-letter word made up of the end of one word and the beginning of the next:

perfect, igloo, knot

Answer

Q115. Find a four-letter word made up of the end of one word and the beginning of the next:

vanquish, Ipswich, climber

Answer

Q116. Find a four-letter word made up of the end of one word and the beginning of the next:

settle, principal, express

Answer _____

Question type 3

Your task is to find the synonym, which is the name for a word or phrase that means the same or nearly the same as another word or phrase. Otherwise you have to find the word or phrase with the strongest connection. But remember, one word or phrase must come from each list.

Two examples:

Find two words, **one from each list**, closest in meaning or with the strongest connection:

Q117. game   snooker ball
       queue   supermarket
       trail   tailback

Answer | **queue and tailback** |

The answers are 'queue' and 'tailback', which both mean a line of, for example, waiting cars.

Q118. guitar   drums
       bugle   gong
       piano   harp

Answer | **guitar and harp** |

In this example the answers are 'guitar' and 'harp' because they are the most similar types of instruments listed (both have strings that are plucked).

Try these examples:

Q119. hold up   delay
       remain   continue
       stop   proceed

Answer | |

Q120. age   leap year
       pensioner   grow old
       clock   calendar

Answer

Q121. pulse   ripple
       flash   flutter
       wave   swing

Answer

Q122. fossil   boulder
       jewel   mineral
       stone   sand

Answer

Q123. luxury   comfortable
       economical uncomfortable
       expensive   give away

Answer

Q124. coins   credit card
       notes   change
       cheques   wallet

Answer

Q125. add   arithmetic
       subtract   divide
       maths   multiply

Answer

Q126. genius   generous
      genuine   glamorous
      genial   gifted

Answer

Q127. cook   roast
      meal   eat
      banquet   devour

Answer

Q128. husband   widower
      bachelor   dad
      father   youth

Answer

Q129. cockerel   tom-cat
      butterfly   duckling
      hen   drake

Answer

Q130. boundary   heart
      middle   brain
      fringe   body

Answer

Q131. beef   lamb
      turkey   chicken
      venison   pork

Answer

Q132. headlight   sunlight
       street light   starlight
       daylight   moonlight

Answer _____

Q133. broad   slight
       grand   splendid
       great   slim

Answer _____

Q134. nickname   first name
       surname   title
       alias   family name

Answer _____

Q135. January   August
       December   April
       July   October

Answer _____

Q136. crevice   drop
       split   smash
       chip   splinter

Answer _____

Q137. flyover   bypass
       subway   viaduct
       underpass   ring road

Answer _____

Q138. peal   drone
      ring   shriek
      buzz   yell
                    Answer

Q139. rough   exact
      stormy   velvety
      approximate   boisterous
                    Answer

Q140. story   tragedy
      comic   romance
      factual   humorous
                    Answer

Q141. signal   commence
      indicate   cease
      begin   finish
                    Answer

Q142. immoral   accident prone
      careless   faultless
      poor   unreasonable
                    Answer

Q143. melody   beat
      tune   harmony
      rhythm   note
                    Answer

Q144. flammable   poisonous
      radioactive   polluted
      toxic   wholesome
                    Answer

Q145. stale   bitter
      appetizing   sweet
      salty   tasty

                   Answer [   ]

Q146. boarding school   secondary school
      primary school   nursery school
      kindergarten   comprehensive school

      Answer [   ]

Q147. sweet   treacle
      strawberry ice cream
      sour   tart

                  Answer [   ]

Q148. unusual   ordinary
      exceptional exciting
      everyday   unsatisfactory

                   Answer [   ]

Q149. devoted   religion
      faith   charity
      hope   compassion

                Answer [   ]

Q150. harmony   harmless
      bashful   painful
      puny   peaceful

                Answer [   ]

Q151. well off   total
        summary   currency
        sum   money

Answer [   ]

Q152. vacuum   suck
        danger   explode
        blow   setback

Answer [   ]

Q153. hot   tepid
        sunny   warm
        humid   spicy

Answer [   ]

Q154. sketch   paint
        frame   delete
        erase   demolish

Answer [   ]

Q155. satisfied   discontent
        dejected   mood
        disposition   relaxed

Answer [   ]

Q156. moonlight   eclipse
        starless   shadow
        dawn   pitch black

Answer [   ]

Q157. dominate   ownership
      seize   grasp
      occupy   liberate

                   Answer

Q158. popular   sparse
      crammed   stretched
      thin   volume

                   Answer

Q159. leisurely   gruelling
      tedious   laborious
      dull   carefree

                   Answer

Q160. ancestry   roots
      beginning   causes
      belong   identity

                   Answer

Q161. forgery   replica
      original   substitute
      copy   development

                   Answer

Q162. inspect   ignore
      test   survey
      dissect   explain

                   Answer

Q163. chart   code
      graph   clue
      display   map

                   Answer

Question type 4

Your task is to find two words, one from each group, which when put together form a new word.

     For example:

Q164. bull   dip
       bulky   dirty
       build   dog

Answer | **bulldog** |

The answer is 'bulldog'.

Try these examples:

Q165. rag   key
       don   still
       ace   vote

Answer | |

Q166. desk   mouse
       build   top
       ache   rule

Answer | |

Q167. ray   day
       Sun   axe
       ace   fad

Answer | |

Q168. bridge   chair
       deck   sofa
       ship   table

Answer

Q169. brief   bag
       notes   case
       assignment   trunk

Answer

Q170. present   dusk
       after   night
       before   noon

Answer

Q171. circle   curve
       loop   round
       ditch   hole

Answer

Q172. head   cap
       foot   flap
       knee   hat

Answer

Q173. pass   air
       stop   port
       go   dock

Answer

Q174. air   barn
        gas   yard
        wind   field

        Answer [   ]

Q175. hard   speaker
        soft   screen
        loud   mouse

        Answer [   ]

Q176. sail   water
        motor   stream
        paddle   way

        Answer [   ]

Q177. plane   fruit
        hammer   berry
        rasp   grain

        Answer [   ]

Q178. low   light
        high   dark
        flat   dusk

        Answer [   ]

Q179. jelly   bird
        cake   fish
        crisp   beast

        Answer [   ]

Q180. pack   time
        horse   age
        load   past

Answer ⬚

Q181. head   lace
        neck   silk
        toe   wool

Answer ⬚

Q182. break   thought
        mend   through
        fix   throw

Answer ⬚

Q183. under   keep
        over   hide
        straight   throw

Answer ⬚

Q184. test   friend
        try   mate
        check   chum

Answer ⬚

Q185. cow   shoe
        sheep   slipper
        horse   boot

Answer ⬚

Q186. for   none
        in   come
        when   some

Answer

Q187. radio   lazy
        wave   idle
        aerial   active

Answer

Q188. fold   bones
        chop   stones
        cut   sticks

Answer

Q189. dead   rope
        alive   line
        wanted   hook

Answer

Q190. hand   wise
        for   ate
        other   ply

Answer

Q191. fun   tune
        cap   tight
        air   take

Answer

Q192. arm   chair
       leg   stool
       body   seat

                           Answer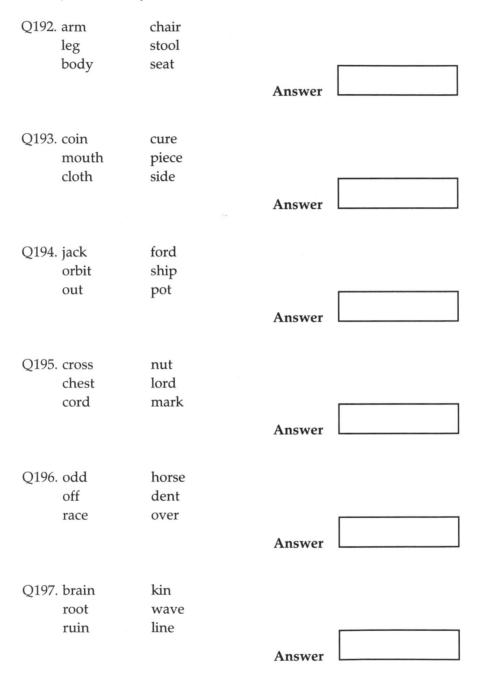

Q193. coin   cure
       mouth   piece
       cloth   side

                           Answer

Q194. jack   ford
       orbit   ship
       out   pot

                           Answer

Q195. cross   nut
       chest   lord
       cord   mark

                           Answer

Q196. odd   horse
       off   dent
       race   over

                           Answer

Q197. brain   kin
       root   wave
       ruin   line

                           Answer

Q198. bull   wide
      nation   lock
      build   cove

Answer

Q199. short   piece
      pepper mint
      shell   room

Answer

Q200. copy   some
      bug   vex
      loath   ward

Answer

Q201. eaves   but
      colour drum
      comb   drop

Answer

Q202. in   certain
      of   less
      an   sure

Answer

Q203. sink   ship
      tube   rate
      friend end

Answer

Q204. dread   out
        scare   full
        afraid   locks

                                    Answer [   ]

Q205. rain   phone
        pill   chip
        side   fall

                                    Answer [   ]

Q206. art   gas
        now   here
        air   bate

                                    Answer [   ]

Q207. draw   script
        size   bridge
        man   line

                                    Answer [   ]

Q208. pin   on
        no   rate
        corn   late

                                    Answer [   ]

Q209. mark   out
        cord   day
        drop   ate

                                    Answer [   ]

Question type 5

In this type of question your task is to find opposites, which are words that are completely different.

For example:

Find the word in the list that means the opposite to the word on the left.

Q210. open   enclosed
                  extensive
                  clear
                  friendly

Answer | **enclosed** |

The answer is 'enclosed', which is the opposite to 'open'.

Try these examples:

Q211. pause   hesitate
                  proceed
                  rest
                  hasty

Answer | |

Q212. choose   pick
                  favour
                  deject
                  reject

Answer | |

Q213. flat   regular
                  uniform
                  uneven
                  unwell

Answer | |

Q214. ruler   monarch
subject
magnificent
devoted

Answer ☐

Q215. proud   pleased
notable
despise
modest

Answer ☐

Q216. express   talk
hurried
slow
idea

Answer ☐

Q217. torment   mock
sneer
circus
respect

Answer ☐

Q218. comic   disaster
magazine
funny
tragic

Answer ☐

Q219. twin   single
              duplicate
              married
              identical

                                    Answer [   ]

Q220. join   link
              mingle
              leave
              obstruct

                                    Answer [   ]

Q221. save   use
              keep
              sale
              economical

                                    Answer [   ]

Q222. chuckle snigger
              roar
              laugh
              cry

                                    Answer [   ]

Q223. mess   jumble
              spread
              clear
              dirty

                                    Answer [   ]

Q224. racket   silence
                    noise
                    bat
                    ball

                                            Answer

Q225. single   lonely
                    echo
                    neighbour
                    double

                                            Answer

Q226. drain   fill
                    sink
                    empty
                    load

                                            Answer

Q227. stay   resident
                    lure
                    defend
                    flee

                                            Answer

Q228. hinder   confront
                    attack
                    help
                    arrest

                                            Answer

Q229. warm   panic
                  annoy
                  icy
                  boring

                                        Answer [   ]

Q230. request   reject
                  seek
                  appeal
                  plea

                                        Answer [   ]

Q231. jesting   witty
                  tender
                  patient
                  serious

                                        Answer [   ]

Q232. badly   well
                  unattractive
                  nasty
                  magic

                                        Answer [   ]

Q233. barren   develop
                  overrun
                  agreeable
                  useful

                                        Answer [   ]

Q234. benign   kind
malignant
ordeal
cheerless

Answer ☐

Q235. blame   reward
tell off
responsible

Answer ☐

Q236. charm   bewitch
assist
repel
captivate

Answer ☐

Q237. cheek   ignore
saucy
upset
respect

Answer ☐

Q238. parent   child
mother
sister
adult

Answer ☐

Q239. begin   return
close
start
initiate

Answer

Q240. agreement   hostility
bargain
deal
dispute

Answer

Q241. achieve   attain
fail
exclude
inferior

Answer

Q242. mild   warm
slack
harsh
acid

Answer

Q243. shorten   diminish
lengthen
moderate
increase

Answer

Q244. lenient   strict
easygoing
hard
unfair

Answer ☐

Q245. active   trigger
still
leave
break

Answer ☐

Q246. increase   lessen
enlarge
climb
mushroom

Answer ☐

Q247. acquire   lose
win
find
buy

Answer ☐

Q248. work   calling
sick
vocation
leisure

Answer ☐

Q249. admire   idolize
prize
despise
regard

Answer [ ]

Q250. legitimate   illegal
untrue
genuine
outlaw

Answer [ ]

Q251. flexible   plastic
supple
adamant
foolish

Answer [ ]

Q252. few   rare
legion
handful
singular

Answer [ ]

Q253. awful   abysmal
unpleasant
horrible
awesome

Answer [ ]

Q254. safe

vault
wholesome
untrustworthy
lethal

Answer

Q255. gorge

ravine
bolt
fast
guzzle

Answer

Practice test

Over the page you will find a test comprising 25 questions.

Use this test to develop your child's test-taking skills. Encourage your child to do the following:

- Keep going if you find the question difficult; the next section may contain some questions that you find easier to answer.
- Make educated guesses at answers and try ruling out possible answers.
- Realize that for some examples of questions you do not need to know what all the words mean to answer the question.

Allow your child 20 minutes to attempt these 25 questions.

Make up more practice tests from the other questions provided in this chapter.

Do not draw any conclusions regarding your child's overall ability or intelligence from the score in this practice test. It is intended only as a source of realistic practice and there is no pass or fail.

Do not turn over until you are ready to begin.

Q1.   What name do you get if you remove a letter from the word 'even'?

Answer

Q2.   If you remove the 'l' in 'land' and 'club' what two new words do you get?

Answer

Q3.   What two new words do you make if you remove a letter from 'tear' and 'seat'?

Answer

Q4.   What letter can you move from 'clean' and 'clap' to make two new words?

Answer

Q5.   What two new words do you make if you remove a letter from 'facts' and 'face'?

Answer

Q6.   Which letter can you move from 'damp' and put in 'hum' to make two new words?

Answer

Q7.   Which letter can you move from 'stringy' and put in 'fair' to make two new words?

Answer

Q8. Which two new words do you create if you move a letter from 'tool' and put it in 'ink'?

Answer

Q9. Which letter can you move from 'page' and put in 'send' to make two new words?

Answer

Q10. Which two new words can you make if you move a letter from 'live' and put it in 'die'?

Answer

Q11. Find a four-letter word made up of the end of one word and the beginning of the next:

fruitful, quota, pelican

Answer

Q12. Find a four-letter word made up of the end of one word and the beginning of the next:

negotiate, arithmetic, important

Answer

Q13. Find a four-letter word made up of the end of one word and the beginning of the next:

machine, India, cheerful

Answer

Q14. Find two words, **one from each list**, closest in meaning or with the strongest connection:

cheerful   miserable
mischievous quarrelsome
wretched   spiteful

Answer [   ]

Q15. Find two words, **one from each list**, closest in meaning or with the strongest connection:

hurry   parade
race   walk
march   stroll

Answer [   ]

Q16. Find two words, **one from each list**, closest in meaning or with the strongest connection:

length   size
weight   width
measurement height

Answer [   ]

Q17. Find two words, **one from each list**, closest in meaning or with the strongest connection:

popcorn   layer
film   cinema
television video

Answer [   ]

Q18. Find two words, **one from each list**, which if combined form a
       new word:

       forward   in
       go   side
       out   top

       Answer [   ]

Q19. Find two words, **one from each list**, which if combined form a
       new word:

       moon   magic
       sun   switch
       star   lamp

       Answer [   ]

Q20. Find two words, **one from each list**, which if combined form a
       new word:

       ice   lace
       snow   bow
       rain   tie

       Answer [   ]

Q21. Find two words, **one from each list**, which if combined form a
       new word:

       voucher   itch
       waist   fabric
       extra   coat

       Answer [   ]

Q22. Find the word in the list that means the opposite to the word on the left:

approve   authorize
       demonstrate
       reject
       represent

Answer [   ]

Q23. Find the word in the list that means the opposite to the word on the left:

surface   area
       middle
       coat
       exterior

Answer [   ]

Q24. Find the word in the list that means the opposite to the word on the left:

minor   younger
       sailor
       junior
       senior

Answer [   ]

Q25. Find the word in the list that means the opposite to the word on the left:

universal private
       public
       open
       illogical

Answer

End of Test

Non-verbal reasoning

This chapter contains over 100 non-verbal questions and provides practice in four styles of question. These are:

■ which shape is the odd one out;

■ the new shape formed when you add two together or take one from another;

■ shapes that complete a series;

■ codes for a new shape when given the codes of example shapes.

The last 20 questions have been organized as a non-verbal practice test.

Both short answer and multiple choice questions are provided. Answers and many explanations are provided on pages 207–214.

Work to ensure that your child is both confident and accurate in answering the questions making up this chapter.

The main benefit of this practice is to help ensure that your child becomes familiar with the principles examined by these questions and learns to recognize the challenge quickly. In many real tests the question involves rotation (where a shape is turned), alternation (where a shape is changed and then changed back), constancy (where a change is made and then must be constantly applied), replacement (where a part of a shape is replaced with another) and attention to detail (where the child must study the shape to distinguish between points of detail).

If your child finds the question difficult then do explain that the real test will contain questions that are difficult and that even the best-prepared candidates will face questions that they cannot answer and will get questions wrong. Practice will allow your child to master questions he or she previously found difficult. When your child has made progress, review some of his or her earlier work and discuss how much he or she has improved.

First there are a few warm-up questions.

Warm-up questions

Q1. Identify which shape is the odd one out.

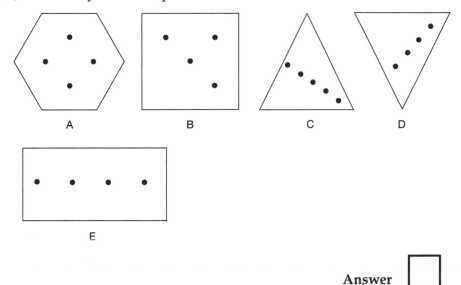

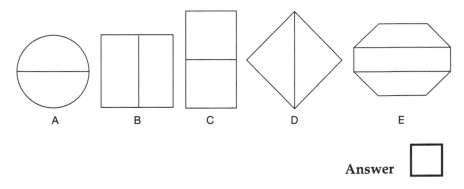

Answer

Q2. Identify which shape is the odd one out.

Answer

Q3.   Identify which shape is the odd one out.

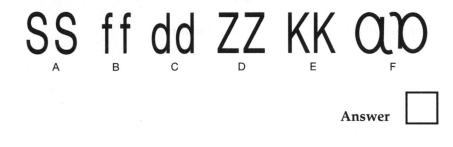

A   B   C   D   E   F

Answer

Q4.   Identify which shape is the odd one out.

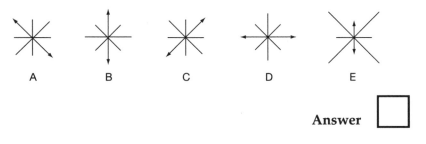

A   B   C   D   E

Answer

Q5.   Identify which shape is the odd one out.

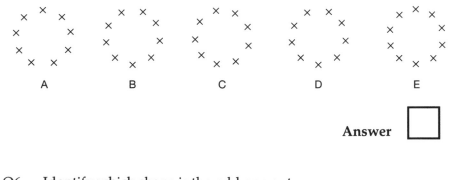

A   B   C   D   E

Answer

Q6.   Identify which shape is the odd one out.

A   B   C   D   E

Answer

A further 24 examples

Q7. Identify which shape is the odd one out.

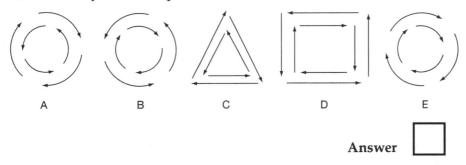

A   B   C   D   E

Answer

Q8. Identify which shape is the odd one out.

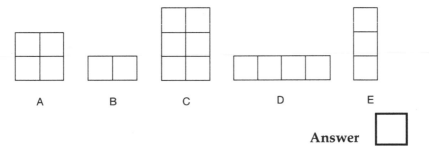

A   B   C   D   E

Answer

Q9. Identify which shape is the odd one out.

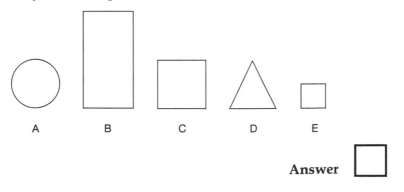

A   B   C   D   E

Answer

Q10. Identify which shape is the odd one out.

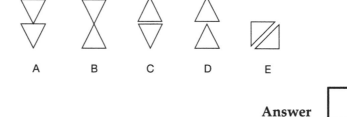

A   B   C   D   E

Answer

Q11. Identify which shape is the odd one out.

A   B   C   D   E

Answer

Q12. Identify which shape is the odd one out.

A   B   C   D   E

Answer

Q13. Identify which shape is the odd one out.

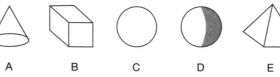

A   B   C   D   E

Answer

Q14. Identify which shape is the odd one out.

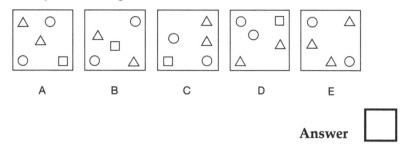

A   B   C   D   E

Answer ☐

Q15. Identify which shape is the odd one out.

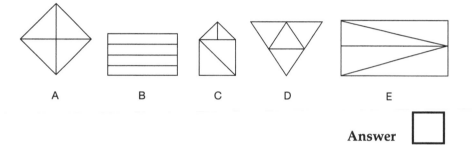

A   B   C   D   E

Answer ☐

Q16. Identify which shape is the odd one out.

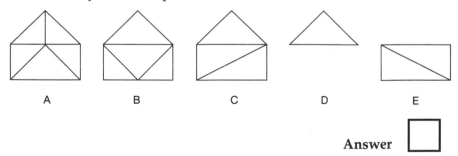

A   B   C   D   E

Answer ☐

Q17.   Identify which shape is the odd one out.

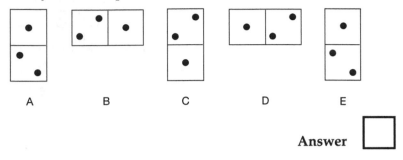

A	B	C	D	E

Answer ☐

Q18.   Identify which shape is the odd one out.

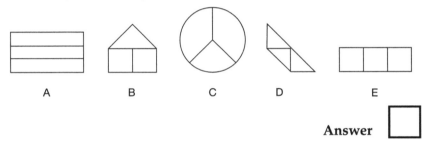

A	B	C	D	E

Answer ☐

Q19.   Identify which shape is the odd one out.

A	B	C	D	E

Answer ☐

Q20. Identify which shape is the odd one out.

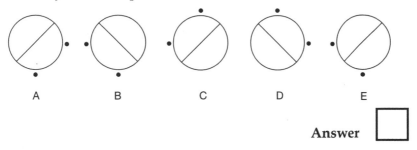

A	B	C	D	E

Answer

Q21. Identify which shape is the odd one out.

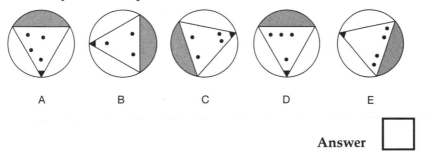

A	B	C	D	E

Answer

Q22. Identify which shape is the odd one out.

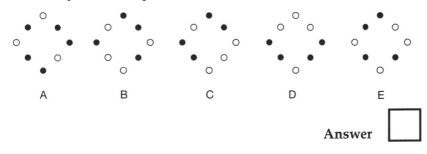

A	B	C	D	E

Answer

Q23. Identify which shape is the odd one out.

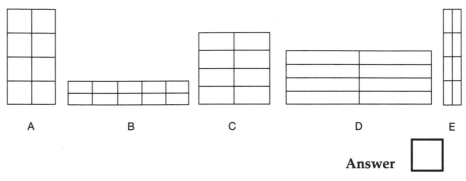

A   B   C   D   E

Answer

Q24. Identify which shape is the odd one out.

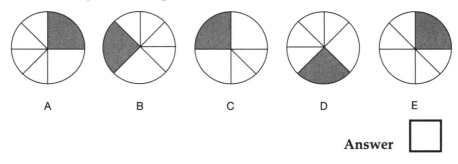

A   B   C   D   E

Answer

Q25. Identify which shape is the odd one out.

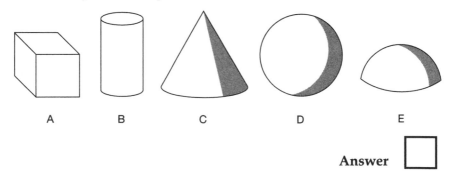

A   B   C   D   E

Answer

Q26. Identify which shape is the odd one out.

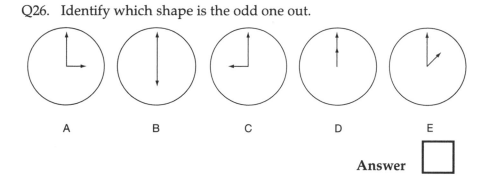

A   B   C   D   E

Answer ☐

Q27. Identify which shape is the odd one out.

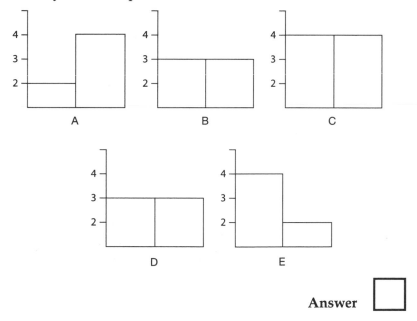

Answer ☐

Q28.   Identify which shape is the odd one out.

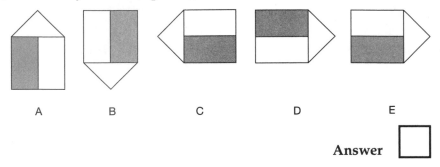

A   B   C   D   E

Answer

Q29.   Identify which shape is the odd one out.

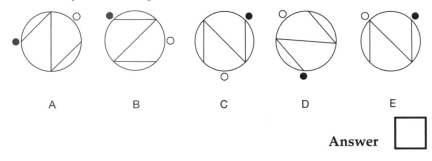

A   B   C   D   E

Answer

Q30.   Identify which shape is the odd one out.

A   B   C   D   E

Answer

New shapes

Identify the new shape formed when you add two together or take one from another.

Q31.

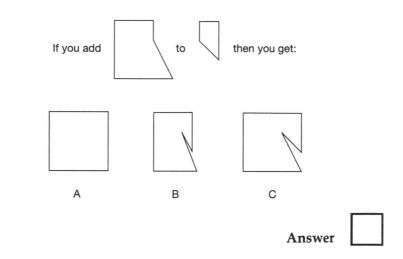

Answer ☐

Q32.

If you add [shape] to [shape] then you get:

A   B   C

Answer ☐

Q33.

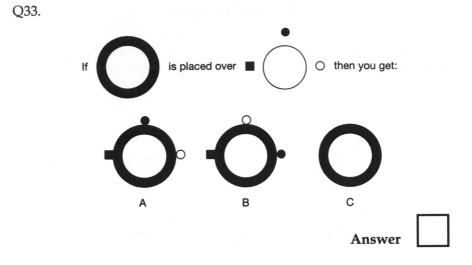

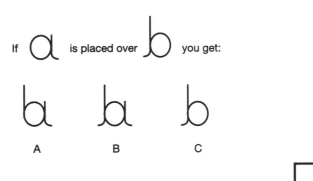

Answer

Q34.

If α is placed over b you get:

A   B   C

Answer

Q35.

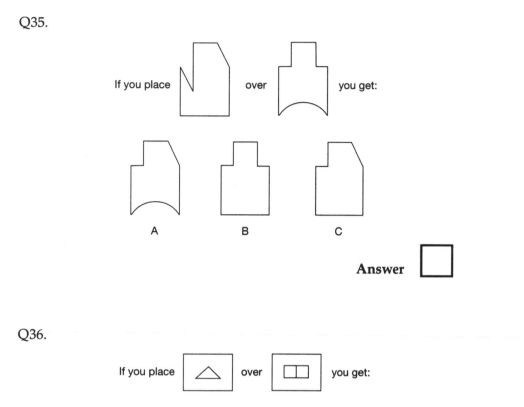

If you place ⬡ over ⬡ you get:

A   B   C

Answer ☐

Q36.

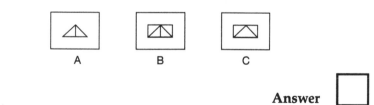

If you place △ over ⬚⬚ you get:

A   B   C

Answer ☐

Q37.

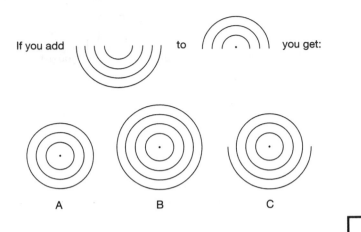

If you add ⟨radiating arcs⟩ to ⟨arc with dot⟩ you get:

A   B   C

Answer ☐

Q38.

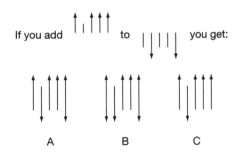

If you add ↑ to ↓ you get:

A   B   C

Answer ☐

Q39. Minus the first shape from the second and identify which of the suggested shapes you would be left with (note that the remaining shape may have been rotated).

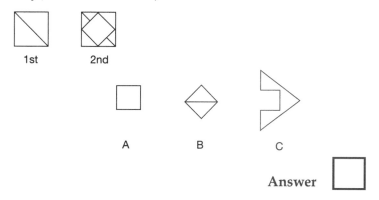

1st   2nd

A   B   C

Answer

Q40. Minus the first shape from the second and identify which of the suggested shapes you would be left with (note that the remaining shape may have been rotated).

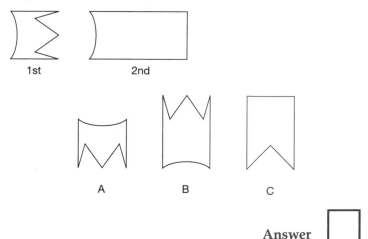

1st   2nd

A   B   C

Answer

Q41. Minus the first shape from the second and identify which of the suggested shapes you would be left with (note that the remaining shape may have been rotated).

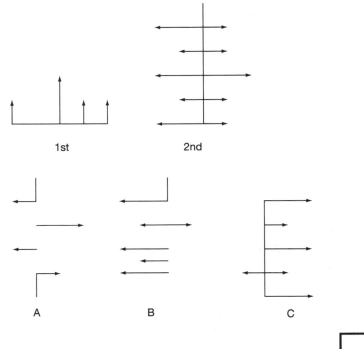

1st   2nd

A   B   C

Answer

Q42. Minus the first shape from the second and identify which of the suggested shapes you would be left with (note that the remaining shape may have been rotated).

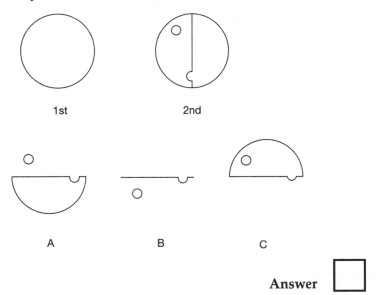

1st   2nd

A   B   C

Answer

Q43. Minus the first shape from the second and identify which of the suggested shapes you would be left with (note that the remaining shape may have been rotated).

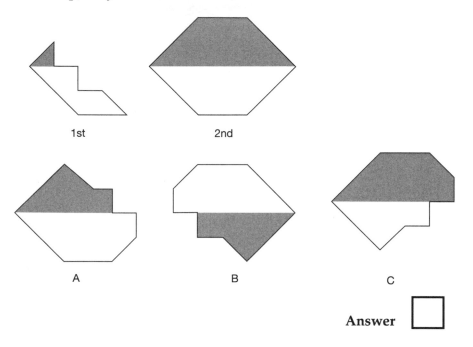

1st   2nd

A   B   C

Answer

Q44. Minus the first shape from the second and identify which of the suggested shapes you would be left with (note that the remaining shape may have been rotated).

         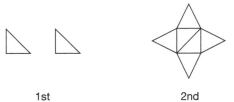

1st   2nd

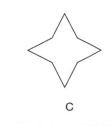

A   B   C

Answer

Q45. Minus the first shape from the second and identify which of the suggested shapes you would be left with (note that the remaining shape may have been rotated).

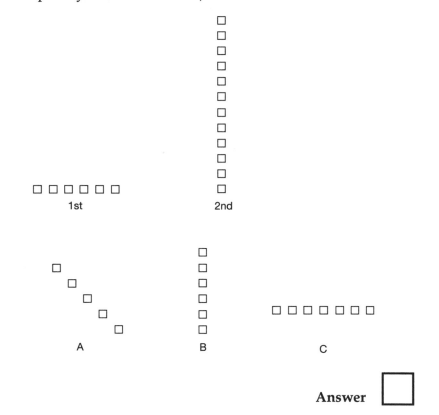

Answer

Series questions

Correctly complete the series in the following 25 examples.

Q46. Find the shape that completes the series.

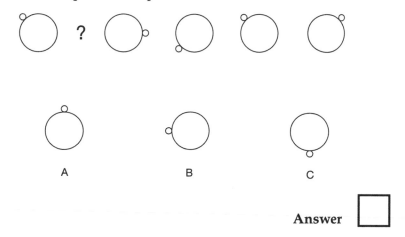

A   B   C

Answer ☐

Q47. Find the shape that completes the series.

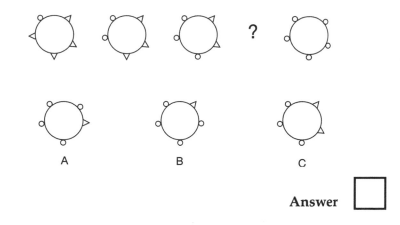

A   B   C

Answer ☐

Q48. Find the shape that completes the series.

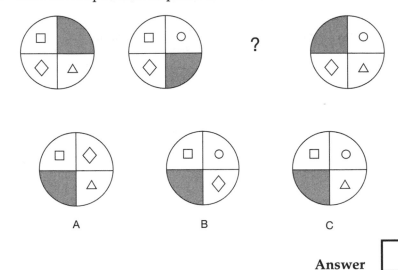

A   B   C

Answer

Q49. Find the shape that completes the series.

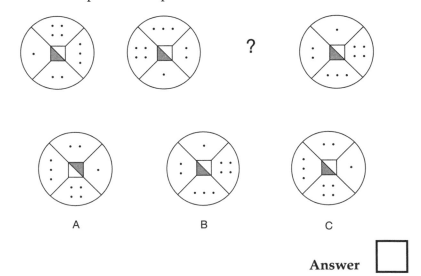

A   B   C

Answer

Q50. Find the shape that completes the series.

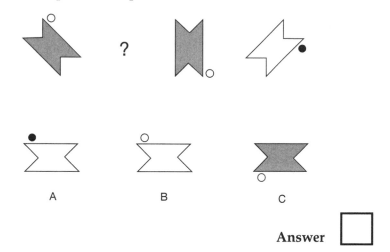

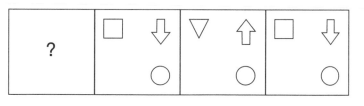

A   B   C

Answer

Q51. Find the shape that completes the series.

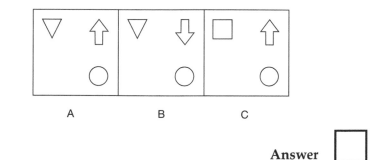

A   B   C

Answer

Q52. Find the shape that completes the series.

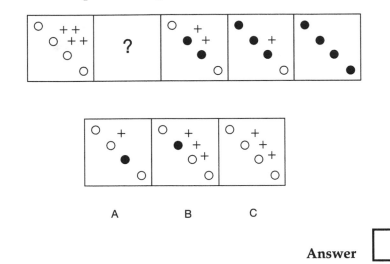

A   B   C

Answer

Q53. Find the shape that completes the series.

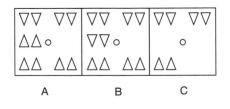

A   B   C

Answer

Q54. Find the shape that completes the series.

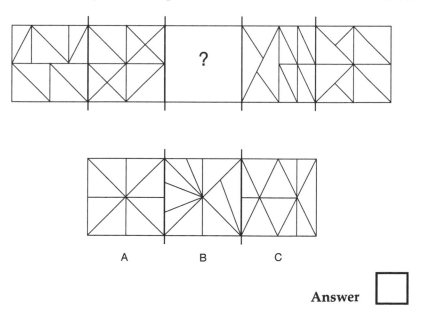

A   B   C

Answer

Q55. Find the shape that completes the series.

A   B   C

Answer

Q56. Find the shape that completes the series.

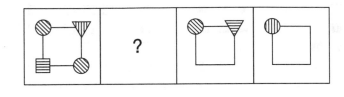

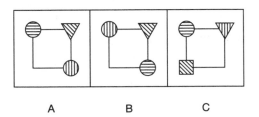

A   B   C

Answer ⬜

Q57. Find the shape that completes the series.

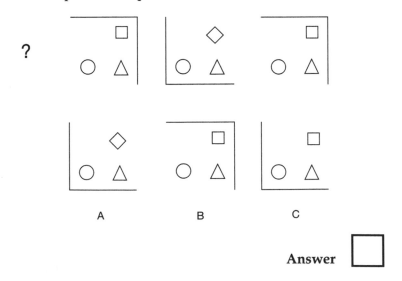

A   B   C

Answer ⬜

Q58. Find the shape that completes the series.

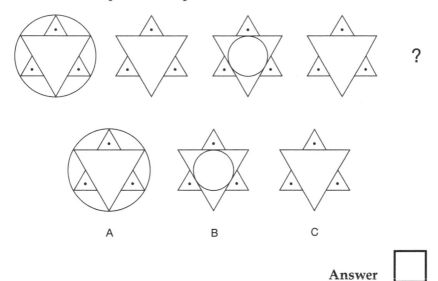

?

A   B   C

Answer

Q59. Find the shape that completes the series.

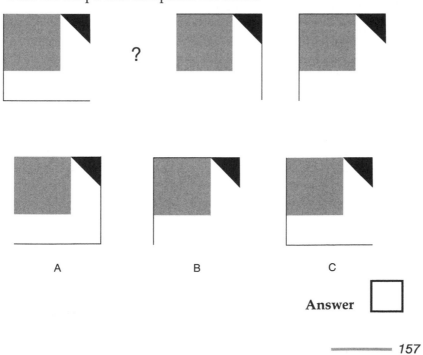

?

A   B   C

Answer

Q60. Find the shape that completes the series.

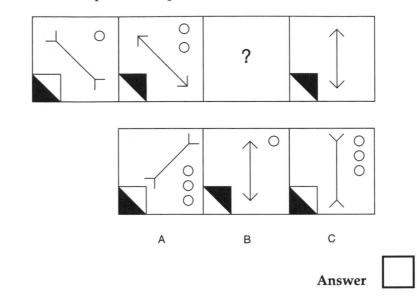

A   B   C

Answer

Q61. Find the shape that completes the series.

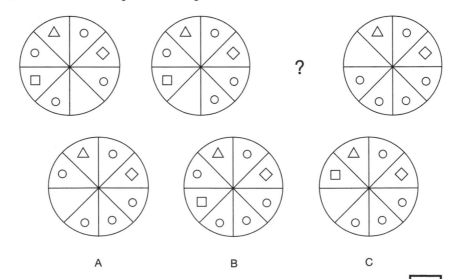

A   B   C

Answer

Q62. Find the shape that completes the series.

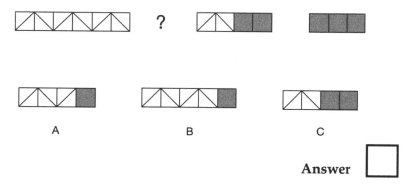

A   B   C

Answer

Q63. Find the shape that completes the series.

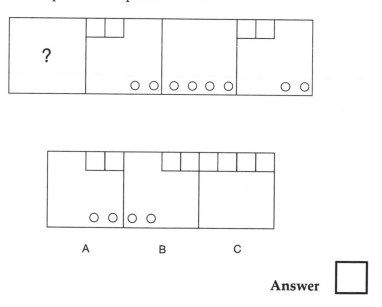

A   B   C

Answer

Q64. Find the shape that completes the series.

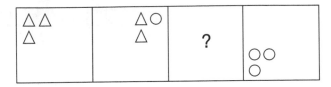

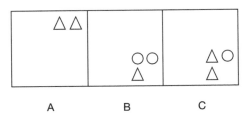

A   B   C

Answer ☐

Q65. Find the shape that completes the series.

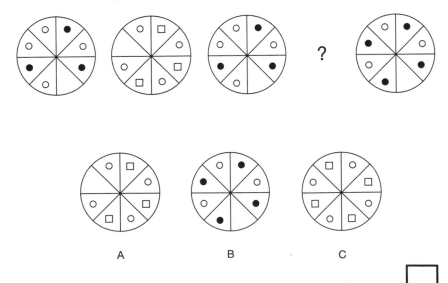

A   B   C

Answer ☐

Q66. Find the shape that completes the series.

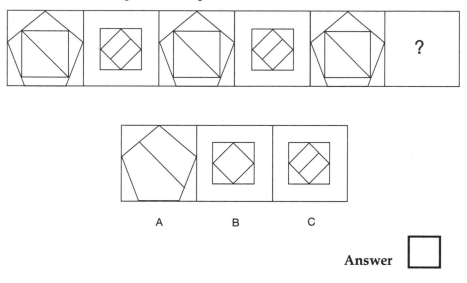

A   B   C

Answer

Q67. Find the shape that completes the series.

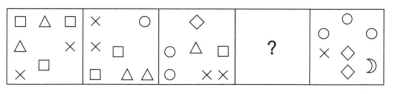

A   B   C

Answer

Q68. Find the shape that completes the series.

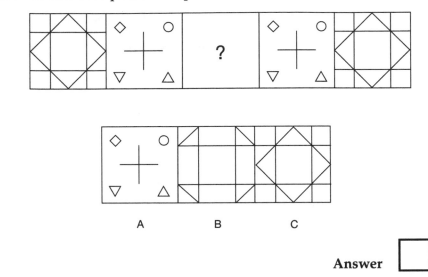

A   B   C

Answer ☐

Q69. Find the shape that completes the series.

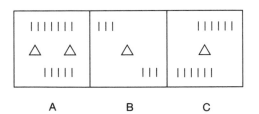

A   B   C

Answer ☐

Q70. Find the shape that completes the series.

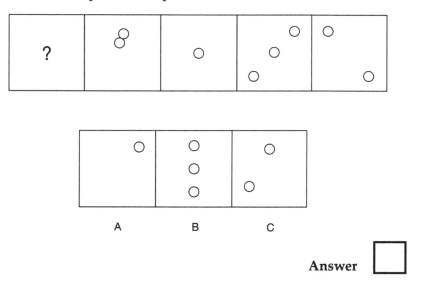

Answer ▢

Codes

Your task is to identify the correct code for a new shape from the codes given for the example shapes.

Q71. Work out the code for the question shape.

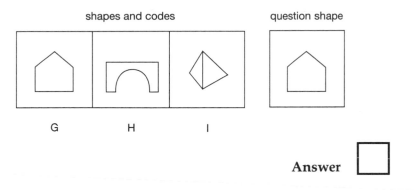

shapes and codes   question shape

G   H   I

Answer

Q72. Work out the code for the question shape.

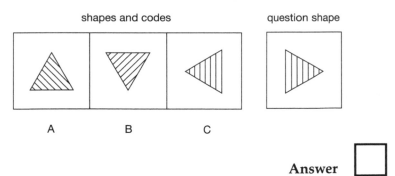

shapes and codes   question shape

A   B   C

Answer

Q73.   Work out the code for the question shape.

shapes and codes   question shape

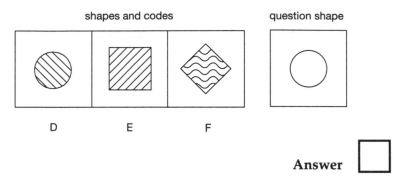

D   E   F

Answer

Q74.   Choose from the suggested codes the one most suitable for the
       question shape.

shapes and codes   question shape

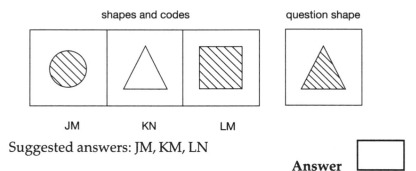

JM   KN   LM

Suggested answers: JM, KM, LN

Answer

Q75.   Choose from the suggested codes the one most suitable for the
       question shape.

shapes and codes   question shape

TQ   SO   SP   TQ

Suggested answers: SO, SQ, TP

Answer

Q76. Choose from the suggested codes the one most suitable for the question shape.

shapes and codes   question shape

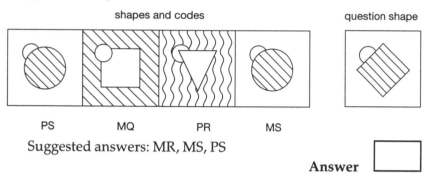

PS   MQ   PR   MS

Suggested answers: MR, MS, PS

Answer

Q77. Choose from the suggested codes the one most suitable for the question shape.

shapes and codes   question shape

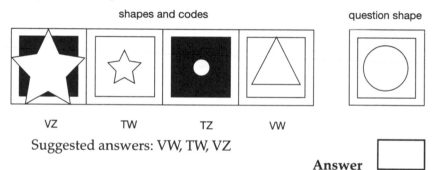

VZ   TW   TZ   VW

Suggested answers: VW, TW, VZ

Answer

Q78. Choose from the suggested codes the one most suitable for the question shape.

shapes and codes   question shape

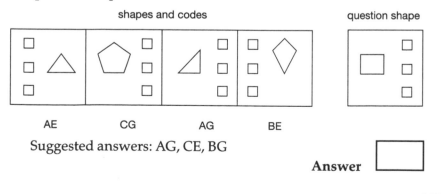

AE   CG   AG   BE

Suggested answers: AG, CE, BG

Answer

Q79. Choose from the suggested codes the one most suitable for the question shape.

shapes and codes   question shape

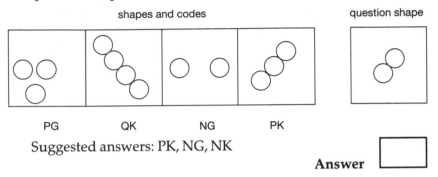

PG   QK   NG   PK

Suggested answers: PK, NG, NK

Answer

Q80. Choose from the suggested codes the one most suitable for the question shape.

shapes and codes   question shape

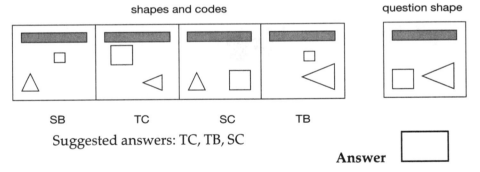

SB   TC   SC   TB

Suggested answers: TC, TB, SC

Answer

Q81. Write the code for the question shape in the answer box.

shapes and codes   question shape

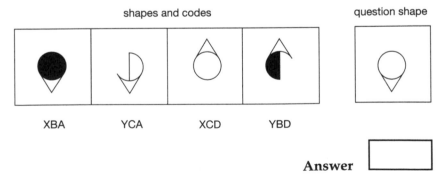

XBA   YCA   XCD   YBD

Answer

Q82. Write the code for the question shape in the answer box.

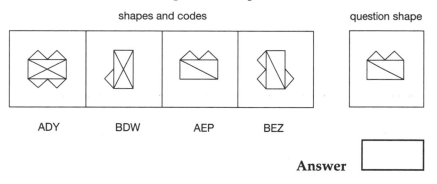

shapes and codes   question shape

ADY   BDW   AEP   BEZ

Answer

Q83. Write the code for the question shape in the answer box.

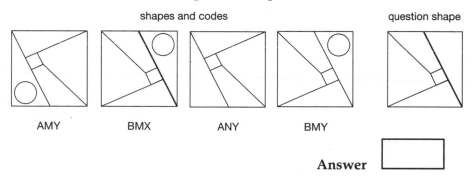

shapes and codes   question shape

AMY   BMX   ANY   BMY

Answer

Q84. Write the code for the question shape in the answer box.

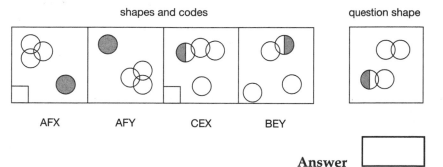

shapes and codes   question shape

AFX   AFY   CEX   BEY

Answer

Q85. Choose from the suggested code the one most suitable for the question shape.

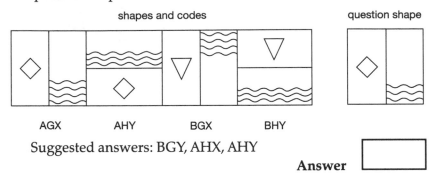

Suggested answers: BGY, AHX, AHY

Answer

Q86. Write the code for the question shape in the answer box.

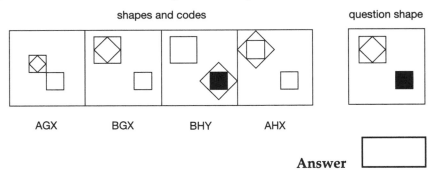

Answer

Q87. Write the code for the question shape in the answer box.

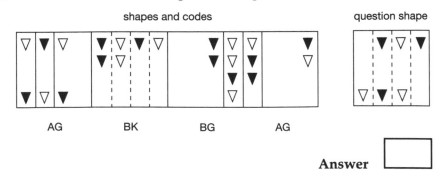

Answer

Q88. Select from the suggested answers a code for the question shape.

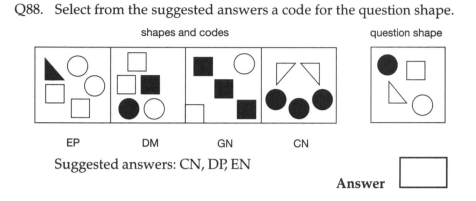

Suggested answers: CN, DP, EN

Answer ☐

Q89. Write the code for the question shape in the answer box.

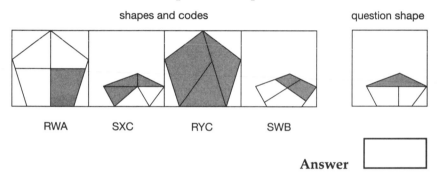

Answer ☐

Q90. Write the code for the question shape in the answer box.

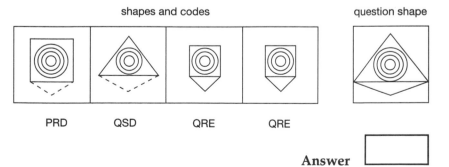

Answer ☐

Non-verbal mock test

This test comprises 20 non-verbal questions.

Allow your child 30 minutes to complete it.

Your child will need a pencil and you should work somewhere where you will not be interrupted.

Use this practice test to develop your child's test technique. In particular:

- Use the suggested answers in multiple choice questions as a guide.
- Do not spend too long on any particular question.
- Keep going if you reach a series of difficult questions as another section may follow that you find easier.
- Work really hard; remember that doing well in a test is as much about determination and hard work as it is intelligence.

Once your child has completed the test, go over the answers and explanations with him or her taking care to compliment your child when he or she has got answers right.

If your child runs out of time then go on to complete any remaining questions without time constraint.

Feel free to adjust the time allowed if you feel your child needs longer or could answer the test in less time.

As with all the practice tests in this book, there is not a pass or fail mark. Simply use the result to identify where more practice is needed. Focus future work on any types of question that your child finds difficult.

Do not turn the page until you are ready to begin.

Q1.

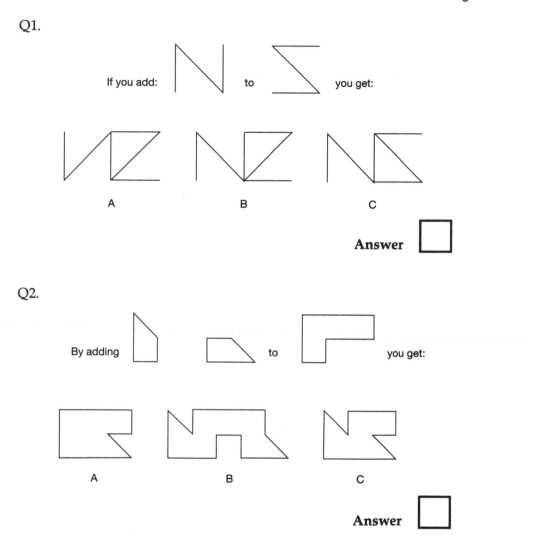

If you add: to you get:

A   B   C

Answer

Q2.

By adding to you get:

A   B   C

Answer

Q3.

If you place this shape ⊕ on top of this one ⬡ what do you get?

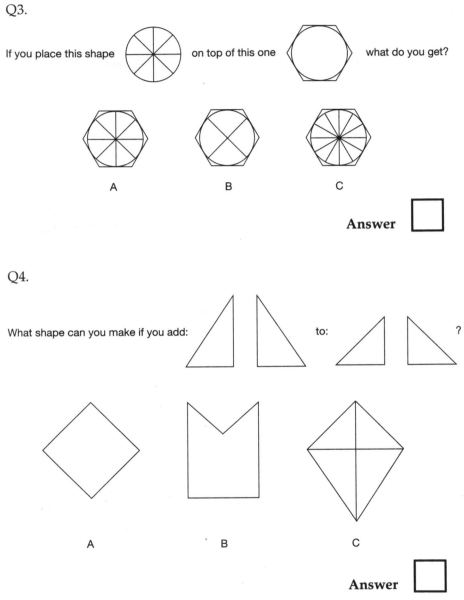

A B C

Answer ☐

Q4.

What shape can you make if you add: ◺◿ to: ◺◿ ?

A B C

Answer ☐

Q5.

Which of the suggested shapes could you make from these?

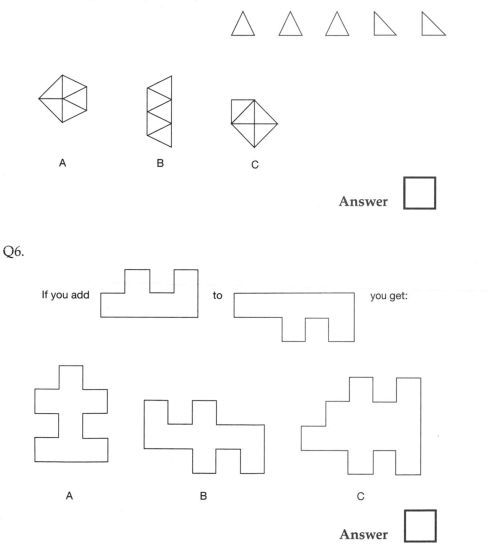

A B C

Answer

Q6.

If you add ____ to ____ you get:

A B C

Answer

Q7.

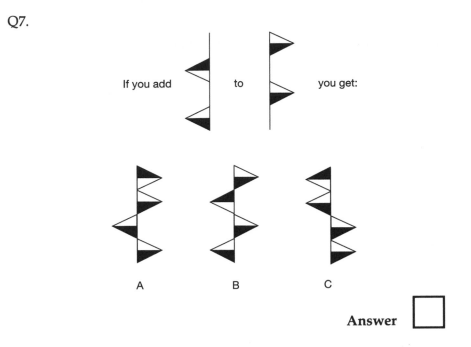

If you add   to   you get:

A   B   C

Answer

Q8.   If you minus the first shape from the second what shape do you get?

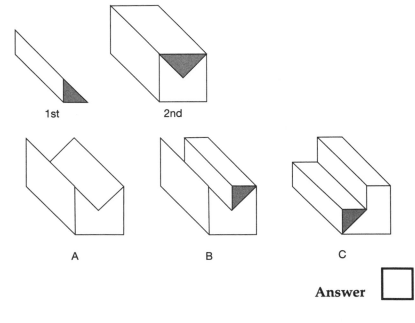

1st   2nd

A   B   C

Answer

Q9.   If you minus the first shape from the second what shape do you get?

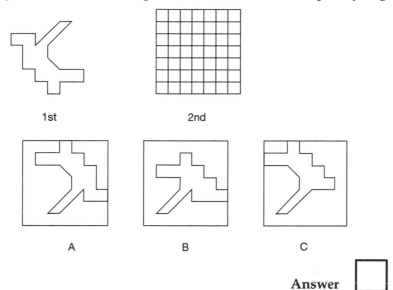

1st   2nd

A   B   C

Answer

Q10.   If you minus the first shape from the second what shape do you get?

1st   2nd

 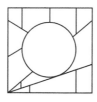

A   B   C

Answer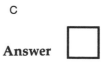

Q11. Which of the suggested shapes completes the series?

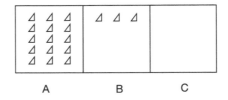

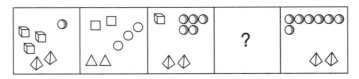

A   B   C

Answer

Q12. Which of the suggested shapes completes the series?

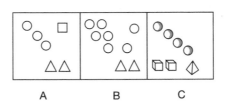

A   B   C

Answer

Q13. Which of the suggested shapes completes the series?

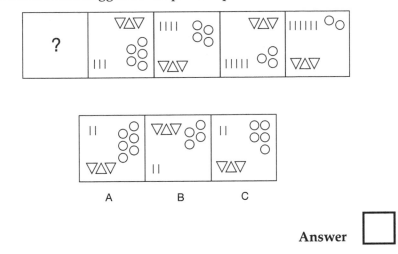

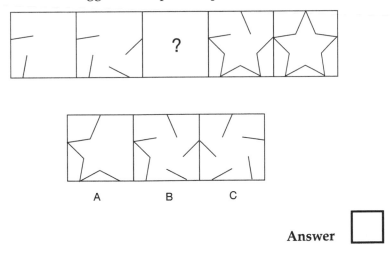

A   B   C

Answer

Q14. Which of the suggested shapes completes the series?

A   B   C

Answer

Q15. Which of the suggested shapes completes the series?

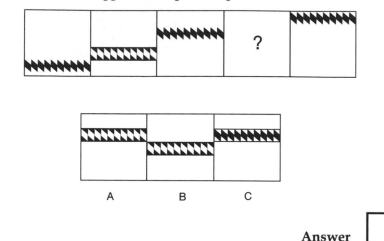

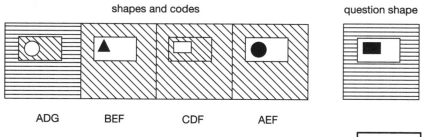

A   B   C

Answer

Q16. Write the code for the question shape in the answer box.

shapes and codes   question shape

ADG   BEF   CDF   AEF

Answer

Q17. Write the code for the question shape in the answer box.

shapes and codes   question shape

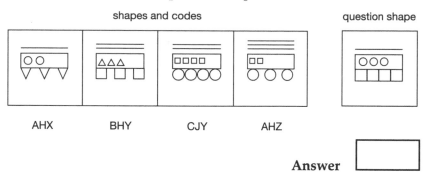

    AHX   BHY   CJY   AHZ

Answer

Q18. Write the code for the question shape in the answer box.

shapes and codes   question shape

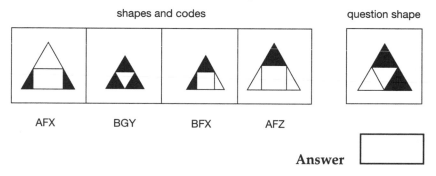

    AFX   BGY   BFX   AFZ

Answer

Q19. Write the code for the question shape in the answer box.

shapes and codes   question shape

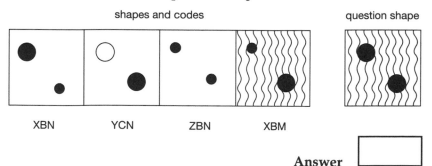

    XBN   YCN   ZBN   XBM

Answer

Q20. Write the code for the question shape in the answer box.

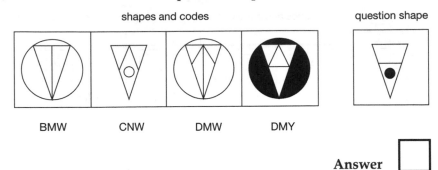

shapes and codes

question shape

BMW   CNW   DMW   DMY

Answer

End of Test

5

Answers and explanations

Chapter 2 Mathematics

A quick test!

Q1. 11.

Q2. 14.

Q3. September.

Q4. Monday.

Q5. 6.

Q6. 15.

Q7. 18.

Q8. 15.

Q9. 16.

Q10. 31.

Q11. 1992.

Q12. 18.

Q13. 100.

Q14. 20.

Q15. 3.45.

Q16. 4 ('a', 'e', 'i', 'u').

Q17. 500.

Q18. Twelve thirty-five.

Q19. 20.

Q20. Saturday.

Q21. 30.

Q22. 15.

Q23. Forty-five minutes.

Q24. 8.

Q25. 2 ('O' and 'I').

Q26. Sing.

Lots of essential practice maths questions

Q1.   299.

Q2.   188.

Q3.   347.

Q4.   689.

Q5.   427.

Q6.   194.

Q7.   665.

Q8.   1,100.

Q9.   6,100.

Q10. 12,800.

Q11. 524.

Q12. 213.

Q13. 91.

Q14. 607.

Q15. 95.

Q16. 428.

Q17. 269.

Q18. 349.

Q19. 179.

Q20. 622.

Q21. 27.

Q22. 30.

Q23. 49.

Q24. 44.

Q25. 208.

Q26. 72.

Q27. 42.

Q28. 12.

Q29. 8.

Q30. 6.

Q31. Answer B.

Q32. Answer A.

Q33. Answer C.

Q34. Answer B.

Q35. Answer C.

Q36. Answer B.

Q37. Answer A.

Q38. Answer A.
Explanation A place value is the value of the numbers in any column before or after the decimal point (think of money). The values run ones, tens, hundreds, thousands, tens of thousands, etc.

Q39. Answer C.
Explanation The .5 represents 5 tenths or ½.

Q40. Highest thousands. Lowest hundredths.

Q41. Answer A = 1, B = 3, C = 1, D = 4.

Q42. Answer D.

Q43. Answer B.

Q44. Answer B, C, A, D.
Explanation Ascending means to go up, so we start with the lowest number.

Q45. Answer D, A, C, B.
Explanation Descending means to go down, so we start with the highest number.

Q46. Answer D.

Q47. Answer B.

Q48. Answer F, C, A, E, B, D.

Q49. Answer D.
Explanation Adding a negative number is the same as taking away. Use a number line to show how adding –3 to –3 involves moving 3 to the left to –6.

Q50. Answer C.
Explanation If you minus a negative number it is the same as adding. Taking away –2 is the same as adding 2. Other examples are –5 – –3 = –2 and 3 – –4 = 7.

Q51. Answer A.

Q52. Answer D.
Explanation On a number line you would start at –7 and move 5 to the left to –12.

Q53. Answer C.

Q54. Answer B.

Q55. Answer B.
Explanation Remember two minus signs next to each other become a plus so the sum becomes 10 plus 8 = 18. Learn the rule and then apply it on a number line.

Q56. Answer B.
Explanation The number line is divided into 4 parts between the whole numbers 8 and 9 so each divide represents 1/4 or 0.25. The arrow therefore points to 8 + 3 × 0.25 = 8.75.

Q57. Answer D.
Explanation The number line is divided into 10ths between the whole numbers and the arrow is pointing to the third. So the arrow points to 4 and 3/10 or 4.3.

Q58. Answer C.
Explanation The number line is divided into 8 between the numbers 0.2 and 0.3. The arrow is pointing at the fourth or middle divide so it represents 4/8 or halfway between 0.2 and 0.3, which is 0.25.

Q59. Answer B.
Explanation To find an equivalent fraction, divide or multiply both the top (numerator) and bottom (denominator) numbers by the same number. To cancel a fraction, we divide the numerator and denominator by the same number. In this instance if we divide both top and bottom number by 3 we get the equivalent fraction 1/3.

Q60. Answer C.
Explanation Divide both numerator and denominator by 4.

Q61. Answer D.
Explanation Divide both numerator and denominator by 5.

Q62. Answer C.
Explanation To find the answer you must divide 480 into 6 equal parts. If your child knows that 6 × 8 = 48 then he or she will realize that 6 × 80 = 480 and that the answer is 80p.

Q63. Answer D.
Explanation Divide 10 into 5 equal parts and count two of those parts. 10 ÷ 5 = 2; 2 × 2 = 4. All the answers are in m² so you do not need to convert this.

Q64. Answer A.
Explanation Divide 63 into 9 equal parts and if your child is confident with multiplication tables he or she will know that 7 × 9 = 63.

Q65. Answer C.
Explanation Divide 50 into 5 parts and count 4 of them. 50 ÷ 5 = 10; 10 × 4 = 40.

Q66. Answer B.
Explanation Divide 60 by 12 to get 5 and multiply it by 7, which equals 35.

Q67. Answer D.
Explanation You know the denominators are 8 and 32 and your child should know that 8 × 4 = 32. As the fractions are equivalent the unknown numerator must also be a multiple of 4. So 6 × 4 = 24.

Q68. Answer A.
Explanation The numerators are 2 and 12 and 2 × 6 = 12. Therefore the unknown denominator is 9 × 6 = 54.

Q69. Answer E.
Explanation 0.125 = 1/8; 0.2 = 1/5. Practise to be sure that your child is confident in the conversion between decimals and fractions. To change decimals to fractions make the decimal the numerator and take away the decimal point. Make the denominator either 10, 100 or 1,000 (ie a power of 10) depending on the number of decimal places there were in the decimal. You now have an equivalent fraction,

which you may need to cancel to its simplest form. Eg 0.5 = 5/10 = 1/2; 0.25 = 25/100 = 1/4. Be aware that some fractions become recurring decimals: 1/3 = 0.333..., 1/6 = 0.166..., 1/9 = 0.111...

Q70. Answer D.
Explanation 3/18 cancels to 1/6 (3 × 6 = 18); 0.2 = 1/5; 0.25 = 1/4; 2/8 cancels to 1/4.

Q71. Answer A.
Explanation 0.125 = 1/8; 12/16 cancels to 3/4; 0.33 is approximately 1/3.

Q72. Answer B.
Explanation 0.3 is greater than 1/7; 3/12 cancels down to 1/4. So it becomes clear that 0.3 is the largest value.

Q73. Answer A.
Explanation 1/2 = 0.5; 2/5 is equivalent to 0.4; and 6/21 cancels to 2/7 and is equal to approximately 0.285. Therefore 1/2 can be seen to be the largest value.

Q74. Answer C.
Explanation To change a decimal into a percentage, multiply by 100. 0.44 × 100 = 44.

Q75. Answer C.
Explanation 0.01× 100 = 1.

Q76. Answer C.
Explanation Percentages are fractions of 100. To find the fraction equivalent, simply cancel down. 25/100 simplifies to 1/4.

Q77. Answer B.
Explanation Change the fraction into its equivalent with a denominator of 100. 3/10 = ?/100. So ? = 30 and 30/100 = 30%.

Q78. Answer C.
Explanation 5/20 = ?/100; multiply by 5 to get unknown numerator; 5 × 5 = 25; 25/100 = 25%.

Q79. Answer A.
Explanation Divide 70 by 100, by moving the decimal place to the left by two places. 70 ÷ 100 = 0.7.

Q80. Answer D.
Explanation Divide 45 by 100 by moving the decimal place two places to the left. 45 ÷ 100 = 0.45.

Q81. Answer A.
Explanation Change all the values into the same expression. Eg 12.5% = 12.5/100, which simplifies to 1/8; 0.5 = 1/2 . It can now be seen that 1/8 is smaller than 1/7 and 1/2.

Q82. Answer C.
Explanation Again we must express all the values the same way. Eg 63% = 0.63; 1/5 = 0.2, so 3/5 = 0.6. The largest out of 0.63. 0.6 and 0.83 is 0.83.

Q83. Answer C.
Explanation To build up confidence in this type of question, try describing the numbers in terms of place values, eg 0.01 = no whole numbers, then the decimal point, no tenths and one hundredth, or illustrate the difference between the numbers on a number line.

Q84. Answer A.

Q85. Answer C.
Explanation Take the next decimal value, in this case 3. As it is less than 5, round the number down to 476.7. If the number in the question had been 476.76 then it would be expressed as 476.8 (rounded up because the next value in this instance is more than 5).

Q86. Answer B.
Explanation You would round up the second decimal value, as the third value is 9, from 2.079 to 2.08.

Q87. Answer E.
Explanation 5 × 5 = 25. Go through the other suggested answers with your child for further practice using the same instruction, eg 4 multiplied by itself is ? = 16.

Q88. Answer D.
Explanation 12 + 12 = 24. Practise with your child this sort of instruction. For example, what

number can you add to itself to get 16 (8), 14 (7), 26 (13), 28 (14)? Answers in brackets.

Q89. Answer E.
Explanation Practise more examples like this until your child is comfortable with the terminology. For example, ask what number you multiply by itself to get 1 (1), 4 (2), 9 (3), 16 (4). Answers in brackets.

Q90. Answer C.
Explanation Break the question down into the two stages, starting with the 36. You are told that something multiplied by 4 gives 36. You can work out what that is by dividing 36 by 4, which is 9. Your child should then be able to recognize the answer to the second stage, that 3 multiplied by itself gives 9. So the answer is 3.

Q91. Answer B.
Explanation Again, start with the known answer 20, divide it by 5 to get 4 and recognize that 2 × 2 = 4.

Q92. Answer A.
Explanation 16 and 12 are multiples of 4. How many other multiples of 4 can your child identify in the suggested answers?

Q93. Answer C.
Explanation 36 and 24 are both multiples of 6. None of the other

lists contain two multiples of 6. How many other multiples of 6 can your child identify?

Q94. Answer D.
Explanation 36 is a multiple of 3, 4, and 6 (3 × 12, 4 × 9, 6 × 6).

Q95. Answer D.
Explanation 48 is a multiple of 6, 8 and 12 (6 × 8, 8 × 6, 12 × 4).

Q96. Answer D.
Explanation 9 × 8 = 72, which means that 72 divided by 8 = 9. Help ensure that your child is confident in using the multiplication tables and uses this knowledge when dividing.

Q97. Answer C.
Explanation 6 × 11 = 66.

Q98. Answer A.
Explanation 7 × 12 = 84. To answer these types of questions quickly, practise the multiplication tables with your child. It takes lots of practice.

Q99. Answer C.
Explanation 7 × 11 = 77. Make sure that your child still recognizes the task when the wording is changed.

Q100. Answer C.
Explanation Help the child divide the task into two stages: first 40 ÷ 5 = 8, then 8 × 3 = 24.

Q101. Answer B.
Explanation 18 ÷ 6 = 3; 3 × 4 = 12.

Q102. Answer A.
Explanation 12 × 5 = 60; 60 ÷ 10 = 6.

Q103. Answer B.
Explanation 9 × 6 = 54.

Q104. Answer D.
Explanation 7 × 11 = 77.

Q105. Answer A.
Explanation 9 × 8 = 72.

Q106. Answer D.
Explanation 9 × 6 = 54. Make up more examples of this kind until your child can confidently answer questions like this.

Q107. Answer C.
Explanation 9 × 4 and 6 × 6 both equal 36.

Q108. Answer C.
Explanation 12 ÷ 4 = 3; 12 ÷ 3 = 4; 48 ÷ 4 = 12; 48 ÷ 3 = 16.

Q109. Answer B.
Explanation Start from the known figure 30, halve it to get 15 and then divide it by 3 to get 5. Go over the sum with the answer to check that it is correct.

Q110. Answer D.
Explanation 100 halved = 50, which divided by 5 gives 10. If your child

finds these difficult, try using the trial-and-improvement method where you take one of the suggested answers, try it in the problem and see if you end up with the given answer. For example, take 5, multiply it by 5 to make 25 and double that to get 50 – this is wrong but it should lead you to try 10 and find the correct answer.

Q111. Answer A.
Explanation This problem is like the previous ones but involves another stage. Again we must start with the known figure 4; to reverse the division we need to multiply the 4 by 12, which equals 48; we then halve 48 (to undo the doubling) to give 24; finally we divide 24 by 4 (to reverse the initial multiplication), giving 6. Go back over the problem with the answer to check it.

Q112. Answer D.
Explanation Starting with 10 we multiply it by 12 to get 120, halve that to get 60 and divide 60 by 6 to get the same figure 10. Go through the problem again with your child to see how it works.

Q113. Answer C.
Explanation Again start with the given, work through each stage

and reverse the signs. $20 \div 5 = 4$; $4 \times 2 = 8$; $8 \times 4 = 32$.

Q114. Answer B.
Explanation If your child is finding these difficult, try taking one of the suggested answers and do the sum to see what result you get; if you do not get the figure 7 then use trial and improvement to find the correct answer. Otherwise arrive at the answer through the following three stages: $7 \times 6 = 42$; $42 \div 7 = 6$; $6 \times 2 = 12$.

Q115. Answer A.
Explanation Use either the trial-and-improvement method or solve the problem going through each stage, reversing the signs and starting with the known amount: $12 \div 6 = 2$; $2 \times 4 = 8$; $8 \times 2 = 16$.

Q116. Answer D.
Explanation $20 \times 2 = 40$; $40 \times 3 = 120$; $120 \div 10 = 12$.

Q117. Answer C.
Explanation The child's task is to find the missing number; in this instance the previous numbers increase by 5 at each step in the sequence so the missing number is $16 + 5 = 21$.

Q118. Answer B.
Explanation The numbers increase by 3 each time.

Q119. Answer D.
Explanation The numbers increase by 12 each time.

Q120. Answer C.
Explanation Each number is multiplied by 2.

Q121. Answer B.
Explanation The numbers are multiplied by 3 each time.

Q122. Answer D.
Explanation Each number is multiplied by 2.

Q123. Answer A.
Explanation Each step is multiplied by 10.

Q124. Answer B.
Explanation At each step the previous number is doubled.

Q125. Answer A.
Explanation Each number is half of the previous number.

Q126. Answer C.
Explanation Add 6 at each step.

Q127. Answer A.
Explanation At each step minus 7.

Q128. Answer D.
Explanation Minus 40 each time.

Q129. Answer B.
Explanation Add 9 each time.

Q130. Answer C.
Explanation Minus 15 each time.

Q131. Answer B.
Explanation The cubed numbers are $1 \times 1 \times 1 = 1, 2 \times 2 \times 2 = 8, 3 \times 3 \times 3 = 27, 4 \times 4 \times 4 = 64, 5 \times 5 \times 5 = 125$, and so on. See the following examples for explanations of the other suggested answers.

Q132. Answer C.
Explanation Prime numbers are numbers that are divisible by only 1 and the number itself. For example, the number 7 can only be divided without remainder by 1 and 7. Try the numbers 2, 3, 4 etc and you will see for yourself.

Q133. Answer A.
Explanation The first few squared numbers are: $1 \times 1 = 1, 2 \times 2 = 4, 3 \times 3 = 9, 4 \times 4 = 16, 5 \times 5 = 25$ and so on.

Q134. Answer B.
Explanation 18 rows and 14 children in each row = $18 \times 14 = 252$ children.

Q135. Answer B.
Explanation There are 3 numbers more than 12 (13, 14, 15) in the bag so the probability is 3/15, which simplifies to 1/5.

Q136. Answer B.
Explanation $14 \div 4 = 3.5$. This means that they need to buy 4 packets and will have 2 sticks to spare.

Q137. Answer B.
Explanation 80 + 115 + 55 = 250; 250 ÷ 2 = 125 or £1.25.

Q138. Answer A.
Explanation The list comprises 2 even and 2 odd numbers so the probability is even or 0.5.

Q139. Answer C.
Explanation 20 × 0.95 = 19. It helps to encourage your child to adjust the amount to more convenient sums. Eg, if you work it out as 95p each for 10 children, this makes £9.50, which you can see is half of £19.

Q140. Answer A.
Explanation 73 × 6 = 438. Undertake more practice if needed at multiplications like this to ensure that your child is confident and accurate.

Q141. Answer D.
Explanation 185 + 220 = 405; 550 − 405 = 145.

Q142. Answer B.
Explanation 300 ÷ 5 = 60; 60 × 4 = 240.

Q143. Answer C.
Explanation For every 3 ice creams sold, 2 are chocolate flavoured so to find out how many this is in the case where 180 are sold we must divide by 3 and then multiply by 2. 180 ÷ 3 = 60; 60 × 2 = 120.

Q144. Answer A.
Explanation To answer the question we need to establish 30% of 270. To do this we can find 1% by dividing 270 by 100 = 2.7 and then multiplying 2.7 by 30 = 81.

Q145. Answer C.
Explanation First find the missing percentage for common dolphins by adding up the other percentages to see how many short of 100% they are (35 + 25 + 25 = 85, which is 15 short of 100). Now we must establish the value of 15%. We are told that 25% equals 30 sightings and from this we can work out 100% of sightings by multiplying by 4, giving 120. To find 15% of 120 we divide 120 by 100 and multiply by 15: 120 ÷ 100 = 1.2; 1.2 × 15 = 18.

Q146. Answer B.
Explanation 12.17 is 43 minutes to 1.00 (60 − 17 = 43); then add the 53 minutes past 1.00: 43 + 53 = 96 minutes.

Q147. Answer D.
Explanation The mean is the average number and is found in this instance by dividing the total number of nuts by the number of types of nut. From the mean we can work out how many nuts there were in the packet by

multiplying the mean by the number of types of nut, so $25 \times 5 = 125$. Having worked this out we can now work out how many hazelnuts there were by adding up the number of other types of nuts and taking that number away from the total of 125. Thus $40 + 30 + 20 + 15 = 105$, leaving 20 as the number of hazelnuts.

Q148. Answer C.
Explanation The total travel time is $20 + 60 + 20 = 100$ minutes. So the time on the ferry is 20/100, which in its simplest terms is 1/5.

Q149. Answer D.
Explanation You can solve this problem in a variety of ways, for example $23 - 11 = 12$ years (this is in how many years' time Carlo's cousin will finish university); $4 + 12 = 16$, which is the age that Carlo will be at that time.

Q150. Answer C.
Explanation $14.00 - 6.00 = 8.00$.

Q151. Answer C.
Explanation To find a percentage increase of 40%, calculate 140% of the initial amount. $30 \times 140/100 = 30 \times 1.4 = 42$.

Q152. Answer D.
Explanation The probability is found by dividing the number of successful outcomes by the number of possible outcomes. There is only 1 green disc so the number of successful outcomes is 1. There are in total 6 discs so the possible outcomes are 6. The probability of a green disc being selected is then 1/6.

Q153. Answer D.
Explanation The mean is the numerical average and is found by adding up the value of all the items and then dividing that figure by the number of items. So $25 + 30 + 20 + 22 + 13 = 110$; $110 \div 5 = 22$.

Q154. Answer A.

Q155. Answer A.
Explanation $500 - 116 = 384$; $384 \div 6 = 64$.

Q156. Answer C.
Explanation Round figures to more convenient amounts in order to approximate the answer. Then look to the suggested answers to see if you can get the answer correct. This way you may not have to spend time on the full calculation. In this instance, the figure of 58 can be rounded up to 60. It is then possible to see that $60 \times 12 = 720$ and that the farmer will need more than 12 crates but that the 13th crate will be only partially full.

Q157. Answer B.
Explanation In 2001 the figure was over 600; in 2002 the figure must be over 1,200 and in 2003 the figure will be over 2,400.

Q158. Answer D.
Explanation 360:120 simplifies to 3:1. If this is not clear straight away then illustrate it with the steps. Start with 360:120; divide both by 2 = 180:60; take away the zeros = 18:6; divide both by 6 = 3:1.

Q159. Answer C.
Explanation To change a fraction into a percentage, first simplify it and then multiply it by 100. 9/12 = 3/4 × 100 = 75%.

Q160. Answer D.
Explanation Calculate the value of each part. There are 5 parts (3 + 2). 100 ÷ 5 = 20. So each part is worth £20. One child gets 3 parts = £60 and the other gets 2 parts = £40.

Q161. Answer C.
Explanation To calculate one number as a percentage of another, you make the first number a fraction of the other and multiply by 100. Eg 2/33 × 100/1 = 200/33 = 6.06. However, this problem can be solved much more conveniently by estimation. If it were 2 children out of 100 then it would be 2%; in this instance it is 2 out of 33 children; 33 goes a little over 3 times into 100 so the percentage must be close to 2 × 3 = 6%.

Q162. Answer C.
Explanation Two-thirds watched the programme; one-third did not. To calculate 1/3 of 165 we divide the total by 3. 165 ÷ 3 = 55.

Q163. Answer B.
Explanation A dice has 6 sides and a coin 2.

Practice real-life problems test

Q1. Answer B.
Explanation There are 10 parts (7 + 2 + 1) so each part has a value of 200/10 = 20. So a 200ml bottle contains 20ml of blackcurrant juice.

Q2. Answer C.
Explanation The answer is found by adding the number of children who did B and D (24% + 8%). The whole sample comprised 25 children so the answer is 32% of 25.

Q3. Answer A.
Explanation It was a close result but Tom obtained the most votes at 15 + 17 = 32.

Q4.   Answer C.
Explanation It rained on 20 days in February and 10 in November so the difference is 10 days.

Q5.   Answer B.
Explanation The probability is found by dividing the number of successful outcomes by the number of possible outcomes. So the chances are 1 in 4 or 0.25. Probability is expressed as either a fraction or decimal of 1.

Q6.   Answer D.
Explanation Take the problem one stage (or ride) at a time: 50 on board for the first ride, 50 – 20 + 15 = 45 on board for the second ride, 45 – 30 + 12 = 27 on board for the third ride, so 50 – 27 = 23 free spaces on the third ride.

Q7.   Answer D.
Explanation 149 – 73 = 76.

Q8.   Answer A.
Explanation 1,280 ÷ 4 = 320.

Q9.   Answer A.
Explanation The total number of children is 25 + 15 = 40. So the fraction of boys is 15/40, which cancels to 3/8 (divide top and bottom by 5).

Q10.   Answer D.
Explanation Sharing the pizza equally means that each child gets 1/6 of the whole. As there are two boys, the boys receive 2/6 of the whole, which simplifies to 1/3.

Q11.   Answer D.
Explanation First work out the cost of a kilo of pears by working out the amount they cost more than apples: $\frac{60}{1} \times \frac{25}{100} = \frac{1,500}{100}$

This cancels to 15. So pears cost 15p a kilo more than apples; 2 kilos of pears then cost 60 + 15 × 2 = 150p = £1.50.

Q12.   Answer A.
Explanation 1. 57 × 12 = 18.84; 15 × 52 = 780. So Allegra gets £18.84 a year interest and £780 for helping in the shop, which when added together give a total of £798.84.

Q13.   Answer B.
Explanation Fay must leave Farlow 3 hours 17 minutes before the flight at 18.44 (1 hour 17 minutes for the train journey and 2 hours for the check-in). So Fay must catch the 15.27, as 15.27 + 3 hours 17 minutes = 18.44.

Q14.   Answer D.
Explanation It may help to break the time down into minutes before the next hour and then the hours before noon and then add the parts together. Eg 7.24 is 36

minutes before 8.00, and 8.00 is 4 hours before 12.00 noon, so the amount of daylight = 36 minutes + 4 hours + 4 hours and 6 minutes (the time after noon to when the sun goes down) = 4 + 4 = 8 hours and 36 + 6 = 42 minutes. So the answer is 8 hours 42 minutes.

Q15.   Answer C.
Explanation £15.00 – £3.03 = £11.97. The three films then cost £11.97. If you divide this by 3 you get the individual costs. Rounding the sum to £12.00 gives £4.00 a film but you then must remember the 3p in total or 1p a film that was lost when rounding the sum. So each film cost £3.99.

Q16.   Answer C.
Explanation 3,000 divided by 6 = 500.

Q17.   Answer C.
Explanation Ensure that your child knows how to move the decimal points out of a sum before undertaking long division. Encourage him or her to change the figures to make the sum a more convenient amount. In this instance you might change the figures to 5.00 and 30.00 to estimate quickly the answer to be 6. Then multiply to check that $5.45 \times 6 = 32.70$.

Q18.   Answer B.
Explanation Be sure that your child reads the question correctly as it asks him or her to identify the incorrect conversion. You can read from the graph that the estimate that 25°C = 57°F is wrong; the answer should be higher.

Q19.   Answer C.
Explanation The total adds up to £5.65, which when taken away from £20.00 leaves £14.35.

Q20.   Answer A.
Explanation Work the problem in stages. For example, work out the time before midnight by taking 2 hours 25 minutes from 6 hours 30 minutes, leaving 4 hours 5 minutes. Now work out what 4 hours is before midnight: 12 – 4 = 8; then take away the 5 minutes, giving you the answer 7.55. Remember that before midnight the time is pm (after midnight am).

Chapter 3 Verbal reasoning

Warm-up questions

Q1. The word 'kid'.

Q2. The word 'rip'.

Q3. The word 'case'.

Q4. The letter 'a' to make 'net' and 'horse'.

Q5. The word 'hut'.

Q6. The letter 'c' to make 'lock' and 'hip'.

Q7. The letter 'd' to make 'fin' and 'ten'.

Q8. The letter 'd' to get 'she' and 'ski'.

Q9. Remove the 'd' to make 'ream' and 'anger'.

Q10. The words 'man' and 'mat'.

Q11. The letter 'g' to make 'low' and 'do'.

Q12. The letter 'h' to make 'same' and 'sake'.

Q13. Remove the 'i' to make 'clam' and 'van'.

Q14. Remove the 'k' to make 'thin' and 'tan'.

Q15. The letter 'w' to make 'arm' and 'ash'.

Q16. The letter 'm' to make 'sell' and 'see'.

Q17. Remove the 'g' to make 'rave' and 'rope'.

Q18. The letter 'l' to make 'pain' and 'pace' or the 'p' to make 'lain' and 'lack'.

Q19. Remove the 'c' to make 'heap' and 'hunk'.

Q20. Remove the 'd' to make 'raw' and 'men'.

Q21. The letter 'e' to make 'stag' and 'sit'.

Q22. Remove the 'h' to get 'air' and 'arm'.

Q23. The letter 'm' to get 'for' and 'far'.

Q24. Remove the 'c' to make 'old' and 'log' or the 'l' to make 'cod' and 'log'.

Q25. Remove the 'd' to make 'ear' and 'rip'.

Q26. The letter 'e' to make 'fad' and 'dad'.

Q27. The letter 'g' to make 'rumble' and 'ruff'.

Q28. The letter 'f' to make 'lower' and 'low'.

Q29. The letter 'g' to make 'sin' and 'host'.

Q30. Remove the 'h' to make 'cart' and 'case'.

Q31. The letter 'e' to make 'pal' and 'past'.

Q32. Remove the 'd' to get 'win' and 'kin'.

Q33. Remove the 'c' to make 'heat' and 'rack'.

Q34. The letter 'l' to make 'pay' and 'pan'.

Q35. The letter 'i' to make 'man' and 'pan'.

Q36. Remove the 'l' to make 'pot' and 'pant'.

Question type 1

Q39. Move the 'l' to make 'and' and 'learn'.

Q40. Move the 'a' to make 'led' and 'mean'.

Q41. The letter 'i' to make 'man' and 'hoist'.

Q42. Move the 'e' to make 'mad' and 'stare'.

Q43. The letter 'r' to make 'bust' and 'trick'.

Q44. The letter 'd' to make 'car' and 'grand'.

Q45. Move the 't' to make 'fain' and 'tart'.

Q46. The letter 'i' to make 'nosy' and 'chair'.

Q47. Move the 'o' to make 'lose' and 'stoop'.

Q48. The letter 'r' to make 'hut' and 'port'.

Q49. Move the 'r' to make 'cease' and 'hard'.

Q50. The letter 'p' to make 'rove' and 'prod'.

Q51. Move the 'r' to make 'cove' and 'learn'.

Q52. The letter 's' to make 'nip' and 'curse'.

Q53. The letter 'r' to make 'fiend' and 'chart'.

Q54. The letter 's' to make 'mall' and 'skip'.

Q55. Move the 's' to make 'gap' and 'smile'.

Q56. The letter 'r' to make 'piece' and 'drive'.

Q57. Move the 'w' to make 'rite' and 'want'.

Q58. The letter 's' to make 'kin' and 'soil'.

Q59. The letter 'y' to make 'luck' and 'silky'.

Q60. The letter 'r' to make 'heat' and 'harsh'.

Q61. Move the 's' to make 'pace' and 'sharp'.

Q62. Move the 'y' to make 'den' and 'dirty'.

Q63. Move the 't' to make 'pan' and 'joint'.

Q64. Move the 's' to make 'kill' and 'slip'.

Q65. The letter 't' to make 'sick' and 'steal'.

Q66. The letter 's' to make 'pot' and 'spray'.

Q67. The letter 's' to make 'lot' and 'sour'.

Q68. Move the 't' to make 'bee' and 'butt' (as a goat does).

Q69. Move the 't' to make 'plan' and 'tread'.

Question type 2

Q71. The word 'reef'.

Q72. The word 'clip' or 'slip'.

Q73. The word 'veil'.

Q74. The word 'need'.

Q75. The word 'seed'.

Q76. The word 'flop'.

Q77. The word 'read'.

Q78. The word 'clog'.

Q79. The word 'peal'.

Q80. The word 'plot'.

Q81. The word 'meat'.

Q82. The words 'span' and 'male'.

Q83. The word 'tear'.

Q84. The word 'also'.

Q85. The word 'owes'.

Q86. The word 'play'.

Q87. The word 'need'.

Q88. The word 'deal'.

Q89. The word 'plea'.

Q90. The word 'stop'.

Q91. The word 'neat'.

Q92. The word 'step'.

Q93. The word 'teem'.

Q94. The word 'leap'.

Q95. The word 'near'.

Q96. The word 'deep'.

Q97. The word 'area'.

Q98. The word 'nosy'.

Q99. The word 'chop'.

Q100. The word 'keep'.

Q101. The word 'dead'.

Q102. The word 'robe'.

Q103. The word 'wave'.

Q104. The word 'moss'.

Q105. The words 'rope', 'open' and 'tyre'.

Q106. The word 'test'.

Q107. The word 'king'.

Q108. The word 'heal' or 'teal'.

Q109. The word 'best' or 'bead'.

Q110. The word 'have'.

Q111. The words 'trip' and 'pens'.

Q112. The word 'vest'.

Q113. The word 'tick'.

Q114. The word 'look'.

Q115. The word 'ship'.

Q116. The word 'pale'.

Question type 3

Q119. The words 'hold up' and 'delay'.

Q120. The words 'age' and 'grow old'.

Q121. The words 'wave' and 'ripple'.

Q122. The words 'stone' and 'boulder'.

Q123. The words 'luxury' and 'comfortable'.

Q124. The words 'coins' and 'change'.

Q125. The words 'maths' and 'arithmetic'.

Q126. The words 'genius' and 'gifted'.

Q127. The words 'cook' and 'roast' (it cannot be 'eat' and 'devour' as they are in the same list).

Q128. The words 'father' and 'dad'.

Q129. The words 'cockerel' and 'drake' (both are male birds).

Q130. The words 'middle' and 'heart'.

Q131. The words 'turkey' and 'chicken' (all are common meats but these are birds and the rest are mammals; the answer cannot be for example 'beef' and 'lamb' because it could equally be 'beef' and 'pork', and the same problem arises for 'venison').

Q132. The words 'daylight' and 'sunlight' (they both refer to light from the sun).

Q133. The words 'grand' and 'splendid'.

Q134. The words 'surname' and 'family name'.

Q135. The words 'July' and 'August' (they are both summer months).

Q136. The words 'chip' and 'splinter'.

Q137. The words 'flyover' and 'viaduct' (they are types of bridge).

Q138. The words 'buzz' and 'drone' (noises that insects make).

Q139. The words 'rough' and 'boisterous'.

Q140. The words 'comic' and 'humorous'.

Q141. The words 'begin' and 'commence'.

Q142. The words 'careless' and 'accident prone'.

Q143. The words 'rhythm' and 'beat'.

Q144. The words 'toxic' and 'poisonous'.

Q145. The words 'appetizing' and 'tasty'.

Q146. The words 'kindergarten' and 'nursery school'.

Q147. The words 'sour' and 'tart'.

Q148. The words 'everyday' and 'ordinary'.

Q149. The words 'faith' and 'religion' (not 'charity' and 'compassion' because they are in the same list).

Q150. The words 'harmony' and 'peaceful'.

Q151. The words 'sum' and 'total'.

Q152. The words 'blow' and 'setback'.

Q153. The words 'hot' and 'spicy'.

Q154. The words 'erase' and 'delete'.

Q155. The words 'disposition' and 'mood'.

Q156. The words 'starless' and 'pitch black' (both descriptions of dark nights).

Q157. The words 'seize' and 'grasp'.

Q158. The words 'thin' and 'sparse'.

Q159. The words 'leisurely' and 'carefree'.

Q160. The words 'ancestry' and 'roots'.

Q161. The words 'copy' and 'replica'.

Q162. The words 'inspect' and 'survey' ('test' and 'dissect' are both invasive).

Q163. The words 'chart' and 'map'.

Question type 4

Q165. The word 'donkey'.

Q166. The word 'desktop'.

Q167. The word 'Sunday'.

Q168. The word 'deckchair'.

Q169. The word 'briefcase'.

Q170. The word 'afternoon'.

Q171. The word 'loophole'.

Q172. The word 'kneecap'.

Q173. The word 'passport' (not 'airport' as one word must come from each list).

Q174. The word 'airfield'.

Q175. The word 'loudspeaker'.

Q176. The word 'motorway'.

Q177. The word 'raspberry'.

Q178. The word 'highlight'.

Q179. The word 'jellyfish'.

Q180. The word 'package'.

Q181. The word 'necklace'.

Q182. The word 'breakthrough'.

Q183. The word 'overthrow'.

Q184. The word 'checkmate'.

Q185. The word 'horseshoe'.

Q186. The word 'income'.

Q187. The word 'radioactive'.

Q188. The word 'chopsticks'.

Q189. The word 'deadline'.

Q190. The word 'otherwise'.

Q191. The word 'airtight'.

Q192. The word 'armchair'.

Q193. The word 'mouthpiece'.

Q194. The word 'jackpot'.

Q195. The word 'chestnut'.

Q196. The word 'racehorse'.

Q197. The word 'brainwave'.

Q198. The word 'nationwide'.

Q199. The word 'peppermint'.

Q200. The word 'loathsome'.

Q201. The word 'eavesdrop'.

Q202. The word 'insure'.

Q203. The word 'friendship'.

Q204. The word 'dreadlocks (not 'dreadful' as it has only one 'l').

Q205. The word 'rainfall'.

Q206. The word 'nowhere'.

Q207. The word 'drawbridge'.

Q208. The word 'noon'.

Q209. The word 'dropout'.

Question type 5

Q211. The word 'proceed'.

Q212. The word 'reject'.

Q213. The word 'uneven'.

Q214. The word 'subject'.

Q215. The word 'modest'.

Q216. The word 'slow'.

Q217. The word 'respect'.

Q218. The word 'tragic'.

Q219. The word 'single'.

Q220. The word 'leave'.

Q221. The word 'use'.

Q222. The word 'cry'.

Q223. The word 'clear'.

Q224. The word 'silence'.

Q225. The word 'double'.

Q226. The word 'fill'.

Q227. The word 'flee'.

Q228. The word 'help'.

Q229. The word 'icy'.

Q230. The word 'reject'.

Q231. The word 'serious'.

Q232. The word 'well'.

Q233. The word 'useful'.

Q234. The word 'malignant'.

Q235. The word 'reward'.

Q236. The word 'repel'.

Q237. The word 'respect'.

Q238. The word 'child'.

Q239. The word 'close'.

Q240. The word 'dispute'.

Q241. The word 'fail'.

Q242. The word 'harsh'.

Q243. The word 'lengthen'.

Q244. The word 'strict'.

Q245. The word 'still'.

Q246. The word 'lessen'.

Q247. The word 'lose'.

Q248. The word 'leisure'.

Q249. The word 'despise'.

Q250. The word 'illegal'.

Q251. The word 'adamant'.

Q252. The word 'legion'.

Q253. The word 'awesome'.

Q254. The word 'lethal'.

Q255. The word 'fast'.

Practice test

Q1. The name 'Eve'.

Q2. The words 'and' and 'cub'.

Q3. Remove the 'e' to make 'tar' and 'sat' or remove the 't' to make 'ear' and 'sea'.

Q4. The letter 'c' to make 'lean' and 'lap'.

Q5. Remove the 'f' to make 'acts' and 'ace'.

Q6. The letter 'p' to make 'dam' and 'hump'.

Q7. The letter 'y' to make 'string' and 'fairy'.

Q8. Move the 'l' to make 'too' and 'link'.

Q9. The letter 'p' to make 'age' and 'spend'.

Q10. Move the 'v' to make 'lie' and 'dive'.

Q11. The word 'tape'.

Q12. The word 'tear'.

Q13. The word 'ache'.

Q14. The words 'wretched' and 'miserable'.

Q15. The words 'march' and 'parade'.

Q16. The words 'measurement' and 'size'.

Q17. The words 'film' and 'layer'.

Q18. The word 'outside'.

Q19. The word 'sunlamp'.

Q20. The word 'rainbow'.

Q21. The word 'waistcoat'.

Q22. The word 'reject'.

Q23. The word 'middle'.

Q24. The word 'senior'.

Q25. The word 'private'.

Chapter 4 Non-verbal reasoning

Warm-up questions

Q1. Answer C.
Explanation The shape has five spots while all the rest have four.

Q2. Answer E.
Explanation The shape is divided into three parts while the rest are divided into two.

Q3. Answer F.

Q4. Answer E.
Explanation The arrowheads are on a short line while all the rest are on long lines.

Q5. Answer E.
Explanation The shape is made up of 10 crosses while all the rest comprise 9 crosses.

Q6. Answer D.
Explanation The shape does not have a shaded circle at one of its ends while all the others do.

A further 24 examples

Q7. Answer E.
Explanation Both sets of arrows go in the same direction.

Q8. Answer E.
Explanation It is the only shape made up of an odd number of squares.

Q9. Answer A.
Explanation All the other shapes have straight lines.

Q10. Answer D.
Explanation The dot moves progressively in a clockwise direction from shape to shape. The odd one out is D because it has moved anticlockwise from the position in shape A.

Q11. Answer D.
Explanation The small squares do not form either a horizontal or diagonal line.

Q12. Answer E.
Explanation This is the only shape made from right-angled triangles; all the rest are isosceles.

Q13. Answer C.
Explanation It is the only two-dimensional shape.

Q14. Answer E.
Explanation This box contains no square and an additional triangle.

Q15. Answer B.
Explanation All the other shapes are made up of triangles.

Q16.   Answer D.
Explanation The shapes form a series in which the number of triangles making up the shapes is decreasing each time, except for shape D, which should follow shape E if the series is to be maintained.

Q17.   Answer C.
Explanation The shapes are rotating clockwise but in C the two spots have been switched to the other side of the shape and should look as follows:

Cut out the shapes and try rotating them to illustrate the point.

Q18.   Answer B.
Explanation All the other shapes are made from one type of shape while B is constructed from two types of shape.

Q19.   Answer D.
Explanation The letters are shown alongside their mirror images except for the 'L', the mirror image of which has been turned upside down.

Q20.   Answer E.
Explanation The dots are moving around the circle one-quarter turn each shape. The exception is E, which has moved by half a turn.

Q21.   Answer B.
Explanation All the other shapes have four spots.

Q22.   Answer A.
Explanation The other shapes contain four shaded circles.

Q23.   Answer B.
Explanation It is made from 10 boxes while the others each comprise 8 boxes.

Q24.   Answer C.
Explanation It has five segments; all the rest have six.

Q25.   Answer A.
Explanation The cube has only straight edges.

Q26.   Answer E.
Explanation The shapes represent the face of an analogue clock and form a series in which the time gets three hours later in each shape. The exception is E where the time shown advances only two hours.

Q27.   Answer C.
Explanation If you add the two totals shown on each graph they add up to 6 in all cases but C.

Q28.   Answer E.
Explanation The shapes have

rotated but the shaded part has moved across the shape in E.

Q29. Answer E.
Explanation The unshaded circle is not at the bottom but at the top of the shape.

Q30. Answer E.
Explanation The 'S' in this case has been reversed; it should look the same as in shape B.

New shapes

Q31. Answer B.

Q32. Answer C.

Q33. Answer A.

Q34. Answer B.

Q35. Answer C.

Q36. Answer B.

Q37. Answer C.

Q38. Answer A.

Q39. Answer A.

Q40. Answer C.

Q41. Answer B.

Q42. Answer B.

Q43. Answer C.

Q44. Answer C.

Q45. Answer B.

Series questions

Q46. Answer A.
Explanation The small circle is rotating around the larger one in a clockwise direction.

Q47. Answer B.
Explanation The arrowheads are changed into circles in an anticlockwise direction.

Q48. Answer C.
Explanation The shaded area is rotating and concealing the shapes as it turns.

Q49. Answer C.
Explanation The shape is rotating anticlockwise around the stationary middle square.

Q50. Answer A.
Explanation The shading is alternating every other shape on both the shape and the ball as the shape rotates anticlockwise.

Q51. Answer A.
Explanation The triangle changes into a square and then back to a triangle each step in the series and the direction of the arrow alternates.

Q52. Answer B.
Explanation The number of shaded circles increases each step in the series while the number of crosses decreases.

Q53. Answer B.
Explanation The number of triangles is increasing by two each time; new pairs are added alternately to the bottom of the shape pointing up and to the top of the shape pointing downwards.

Q54. Answer A.
Explanation The number of shaded squares is decreasing by three each step of the series.

Q55. Answer B.
Explanation The triangles are arranged in a different pattern each time but the number of triangles is alternating from 10 to 12 triangles each step of the series.

Q56. Answer A.
Explanation The shapes are being removed in an anticlockwise direction.

Q57. Answer A.
Explanation The 'L' shape is rotating in an anticlockwise direction and the diamond changes into a square and then changes back into a diamond through the series.

Q58. Answer A.
Explanation Every second step in the series the circle is alternating from big (with the shape inside it) to small (when it appears inside the shape).

Q59. Answer A.
Explanation The 'L' shape is rotating in an anticlockwise direction.

Q60. Answer C.
Explanation The number of circles is increasing through the series 0, 1, 2, 3, 0, the arrowheads are reversing and when the shape repeats it turns in a clockwise direction.

Q61. Answer A.
Explanation The obscured part of the pie is rotating clockwise and as it passes changes all shapes into circles (if they were not circles already).

Q62. Answer B.
Explanation At each step in the series two triangles are transformed into a shaded square.

Q63. Answer C.
Explanation Starting with squares, at each step two are turned into circles and relocate to the bottom; once all the squares have been changed they start turning back into squares (still two at a time) and relocate back to the top.

Q64. Answer B.
Explanation Triangles are being transformed into circles and the group of shapes is rotating clockwise.

Q65. Answer A.
Explanation The obscured part of the pie alternates between two positions while the pattern of shapes is also alternating.

Q66. Answer C.
Explanation The two shapes alternate.

Q67. Answer A.
Explanation At each stage of the series, starting with squares, shapes are transformed, with squares becoming circles, triangles becoming diamonds, and crosses becoming half-moons. Initially a single square becomes a circle, then another square becomes a circle and a triangle becomes a diamond, and so on.

Q68. Answer C.
Explanation The two shapes are repeated in the series, one twice and the other three times.

Q69. Answer C.
Explanation At each step three lines are used to make a triangle.

Q70. Answer B.
Explanation Randomly placed circles are counting down the series 3, 2, 1.

Codes

Q71. Answer G.

Q72. Answer C.

Q73. Answer D.

Q74. Answer KM.
Explanation The diagonal shading and the letter 'M' are repeated so 'M' must refer to this style of shading. The triangle shapes could be represented by either letter 'K' or letter 'N' but only the combination 'KM' is offered in the suggested answers.

Q75. Answer SO.
Explanation The 'S' relates to the direction of the arrow and the 'O' to the number of shapes not the type or location.

Q76. Answer PS.
Explanation 'P' refers to a partially covered circle, and 'S' to shading inside the shape. The type of shape or style of shading is irrelevant.

Q77. Answer VW.
Explanation 'V' refers to a large shape and 'W' to an unshaded background.

Q78. Answer BG.
Explanation A four-sided shape is coded with a 'B', and three squares on the right are coded 'G'.

Q79. Answer NK.
Explanation Adjoining circles are represented by the code 'K'; 'N' is code for two circles.

Q80. Answer TC.
Explanation A big square is coded with the letter 'C'; an arrow pointing to the left (whatever its size) is coded with the letter 'T'.

Q81. Answer XCA.
Explanation A circle is coded 'X', a semicircle 'Y', shading 'B', no shading 'C', an arrow shape pointing downwards 'A' and an arrow shape pointing upwards 'D'.

Q82. Answer AEP.
Explanation When the oblong is horizontal it is coded with the letter 'A', and when upright with the letter 'B'. One diagonal line is coded 'E', and two 'D'. Four triangles around the edge of the oblong are coded 'Y', three triangles 'Z', two triangles 'P' and one triangle 'W'.

Q83. Answer BNX.
Explanation Notice the right-angled triangle that is either in the top right-hand or bottom left-hand corner. When it is in the top right-hand corner it is coded 'B'. When a circle is found inside the right-angled triangle it is coded 'M', and when there is no circle it is coded 'N'. When the hypotenuse is a thick line it is coded 'X'.

Q84. Answer CEY.
Explanation Think segments, not circles or shapes. When the overlapping circles create two segments this is coded 'C', when the shading forms a semicircle it is coded 'E' and when no square is found in the left-hand corner it is coded 'Y'.

Q85. Answer AHX.
Explanation A diamond is signified by the letter 'A', three wavy lines by the letter 'H', and when the box is divided longways it is coded 'X'.

Q86. Answer BGY.
Explanation Think squares flat on one surface rather than on an edge. A large and small square both on a flat side are coded 'B'; a square on its corner inside the other square is coded 'G' (outside 'H'); when the bottom right-hand square is shaded it is coded 'Y'.

Q87. Answer BK.
Explanation Starting from the top, 'B' signifies alternately shaded arrowheads moving left to right starting with a shaded arrowhead. Broken dividing lines are coded 'K'.

Q88. Answer DP.
Explanation Given the suggested answers, 'D' is the code for three unshaded shapes and 'P' for a single shaded shape.

Q89. Answer SYA.
Explanation 'S' signifies a small hexagon, 'Y' signifies that the hexagon is divided into three segments, and 'A' is code for one shaded segment.

Q90. Answer PSE.
Explanation Four rings are signified by the letter 'P', a surrounding triangle by the letter 'S' and a triangle shape made of unbroken lines by the letter 'E'.

Non-verbal mock test

Q1. Answer C.

Q2. Answer B.

Q3. Answer A.
Explanation Make sure that your child carefully counts the segments.

Q4. Answer C.

Q5. Answer A.
Explanation The answer must be made from three isosceles triangles and two right-angled triangles.

Q6. Answer C.

Q7. Answer B.

Q8. Answer B.
Explanation The piece is too small to remove the whole shaded area.

Q9. Answer A.

Q10. Answer A.

Q11. Answer C.
Explanation The triangles are increasing according to the 3 times table, which starts with $3 \times 0 = 0$.

Q12. Answer B.
Explanation The shapes alternate between their three- and two-dimensional representations. At each step in the series a cube or square turns into two circles or spheres. The number of pyramids or triangles remains the same but they move from the left to the right.

Q13. Answer A.
Explanation The number of lines increases by one each move; the circles decrease by one; the number of triangles remains the same. Lines and circles alternate top and bottom; the triangles alternate diagonally.

Q14. Answer B.
Explanation The star is built by adding two lines each move in the

213

series in an anticlockwise direction, adding lines to alternate arms of the star.

Q15.   Answer A.
Explanation The shading is alternating and the pattern is moving consistently upwards.

Q16.   Answer CEG.
Explanation Horizontal shading is coded 'G', a small square is coded 'C' and shading of the smallest shape is coded 'E'.

Q17.   Answer BJX.
Explanation It is the number of shapes not the type that is coded. Three shapes inside the oblong are coded 'B', four along the bottom

'J', and one line over the oblong 'X'.

Q18.   Answer AGX.
Explanation 'A' signifies a large triangle, 'G' a triangle inside, and 'X' that two segments are shaded.

Q19.   Answer YBM.
Explanation Two large circles are coded Y, shading in both is coded B and a wavy background is coded M.

Q20.   Answer BNY.
Explanation A triangle divided into two segments is signified by the letter 'B'; 'N' signifies a circle within the one segment; 'Y' signifies that the circle is shaded.

Sources of further practice material

NFER-Nelson Go Practice! Series (www.gopractice.co.uk)

The Learning Together Series (www.learningtogether.co.uk)

Athey Educational Series Secondary Selection Portfolio (1994)

Further reading from Kogan Page

Other titles in the testing series

The Advanced Numeracy Test Workbook, Mike Bryon, 2003

Aptitude, Personality & Motivation Tests, Jim Barrett, 2004

The Aptitude Test Workbook, Jim Barrett, 2003

Career, Aptitude and Selection Tests, Jim Barrett, 1998

How to Master Personality Questionnaires, 2nd edn, Mark Parkinson, 2000

How to Master Psychometric Tests, 2nd edn, Mark Parkinson, 2000

How to Pass Advanced Aptitude Tests, Jim Barrett, 2002

How to Pass Advanced Numeracy Tests, Mike Bryon, 2002

How to Pass Graduate Psychometric Tests, 2nd edn, Mike Bryon, 2001

How to Pass Numeracy Tests, 2nd edn, Harry Tolley and Ken Thomas, 2000

How to Pass Professional-level Psychometric Tests, Sam Al-Jajjoka, 2001

How to Pass Selection Tests, 2nd edn, Mike Bryon and Sanjay Modha, 1998

How to Pass Technical Selection Tests, Mike Bryon and Sanjay Modha, 1993

How to Pass the Civil Service Qualifying Tests, 2nd edn, Mike Bryon, 2003

How to Pass New Police Selection System, Harry Tolley, Catherine Tolley and Billy Hodge, 1997

How to Pass Verbal Reasoning Tests, Harry Tolley and Ken Thomas, 2000

How to Succeed at an Assessment Centre, Harry Tolley and Bob Wood, 2001

IQ and Psychometric Tests, Philip Carter, 2004

Test Your Creative Thinking, Lloyd King, 2003

Test Your IQ, Ken Russell and Philip Carter, 2000

Test Your Own Aptitude, 3rd edn, Jim Barrett and Geoff Williams, 2003

The Times Book of IQ Tests – Book Four, Ken Russell and Philip Carter, 2004

The Times Book of IQ Test – Book Three, Ken Russell and Philip Carter, 2003

The Times Book of IQ Tests – Book Two, Ken Russell and Philip Carter, 2002

The Times Book of IQ Tests – Book One, Ken Russell and Philip Carter, 2001

CD ROM

The Times Testing Series – Brain Teasers, Volume 1, 2002

The Times Testing Series – Psychometric Tests, Volume 1, 2002

The Times Testing Series – Test Your Aptitude, Volume 1, 2002

The Times Testing Series – Test Your IQ, Volume 1, 2002

The above titles are available from all good bookshops. For further information, please contact the publisher at the following address:

Kogan Page Limited
120 Pentonville Road
London N1 9JN
Tel: 020 7278 0433
Fax: 020 7837 6348
www.kogan-page.co.uk